CW00816055

LAPWING & FOX

Conversations between
John Berger and John Christie

John Christie
2016

OBJECTIF 2016

Previous collaborations:

Another Way of Telling (1988) John Berger and Jean Mohr – four-part BBC television series
Pages of the Wound: Poems, Drawings, Photographs 1956-94 (1994) John Berger
I Send You This Cadmium Red: a correspondence between John Berger and John Christie (2000)
Cuatro horizontes (2015) John Berger, Sister Telchilde Hinkley, Sister Lucia Kuppens and John Christie
– on Le Corbusier's chapel at Ronchamp. Editorial Gustavo Gili, SL

Contents

from John Christie January 2011

Surrounded by faces

Dear John

I thought I would take you on a visit to a
favourite place of mine, the Sainsbury Centre, on
the outskirts of Norwich. It's a gallery I often
visit, a wonderful mix of paintings, sculpture,
drawings and objects collected over a lifetime by
Robert and Lisa Sainsbury. I've made you this small
book with gallery postcards and photos I took on
my last visit to give you an idea of the place –
I hope one day we will go there together.

The collection is housed in part of an elegantly
detailed, hi-tech building designed by Norman
Foster in 1973. It still looks good 40 years later.

There are always changing exhibitions but the
highlight for me is the permanent collection and
if we were walking in there now I would steer you,
trying not to be distracted by any of the other
works around us, through the series of spaces,
created by free-standing screens.

We would pass works by Bacon, Modigliani, Rouault,
Picasso, Degas and Moore, as well as a wealth of
Egyptian and Roman artefacts, masks and ritual
objects from around the world to the picture that I
always gravitate towards, Giacometti's self-
portrait. I first saw this drawing in 1965 in his
Tate retrospective. It was reproduced more or less
full size on the cover of the catalogue. I found a
note in the back of my copy giving the date I went
to the show, 23rd August. When we moved to Suffolk
in 2006 I found the drawing again, permanently on
display and only about an hour's drive away.

You'd be aware too of the other works that surround
you as you stand looking at the drawing; to the
left a 1930s Bomberg self-portrait, behind you a
rather restrained Soutine painting, 'Lady in blue',

giacometti - self-portrait

Bomberg 1930

Giacometti 1935

Egypt - c 1200 Bc

Soutine c. 1931

on either side of the Bomberg and Giacometti are
some small wooden Egyptian figures, housed under
glass, and behind you to the right, about 20 feet
away, a Fayun mummy portrait of a young man from
around AD100.

So you are surrounded by eyes and perhaps it is
the eyes that draw me to the Giacometti every time.

Egypt c.2200 BC

Egypt c 100AD

With just a pencil and a rubber, he has made an
hypnotic image. I've looked hard at this drawing
many times, standing the same distance from it
that he stood when he drew it in 1935. I guess the
mirror which he must have used to interrogate his
face was probably slightly off to the left of his
drawing board because he drew with his right hand.
When you are looking at the drawing your eyes are
where his eyes were.

Several things are striking and puzzling about this
work. Although sections of it are undefined,
because of the erasing, it has a very solid look to
it, as though it's a drawing of a sculpted head. His
wiry hair is a helmet, the ears just outline shapes,
his left eye almost illegible, the remains of the
drawing of his right eye stares directly at you.
He gazes unblinking into the mirror at himself.

Inspecting the face close-up you notice the
reference marks, either hard dots where his pencil
lead rested or the short double strokes he placed
at points over the surface; the neck, the hairline,
the eye, the lips...etc. I tried covering up one
side of the face and a curious thing happens. His
right side fixes you with that slightly severe,
direct look which is defined and emphasised by the
down-turned mouth. His left side is more ambiguous,
especially on the actual drawing rather than in a
photo of it, because it can either look like the
closed lid of a man asleep or the faint image of
his open eye looking away from you to his left.

I went back to the gallery this morning to look
again at the drawing — to see why I found this
left eye - open/closed - so confused in my
memory. On the actual drawing the eye is
open and much less distinct than it appears
on the postcard — a very faint image but
still just visible. I wondered why Giacometti

Alberto Giacometti 1935

didn't erase the eye altogether as he seemed
well on the way to doing so - a few more
strokes of the rubber would have done it
Then it dawned on me that this ambiguity
creates a real tension and life in the
drawing - the direct stare dominates
the image but when you transfer your
gaze to look at the other eye, expecting
the same direct stare, Giacometti is
looking away.

I've watched footage of Giacometti talking and
working (there's a good selection of clips on the
internet) and he seems to have, in life, an open
face with a faint smile about the lips. But it
doesn't seem so in this drawing; here the face
feels to me like a wall. It is the end of that
'narrow corridor of looking between you' which you
describe, in your essay written just after he died
in 1966. Perhaps it feels like an end because he
is looking at a reflection of himself.

It was also a self-portrait made in the year when
he resumed modelling from nature after recently
being excluded by Breton from the Surrealist
group, a time when many friends, because of the
split, distanced themselves from him.

Giacometti made these observations:

'One day when I was drawing a young girl, I
suddenly noticed that the only thing that was
alive was her gaze. The rest of her head meant no
more to me than the skull of a dead man.'

'I knew that one day – no matter how it came about
or what I was working towards, I would be forced
to sit down on a stool before a model and copy
what I saw. And with no hope of succeeding.'

Perhaps this anticipated failure before the object
(even his own reflection) accounts for the erasing,
or partial erasing, of areas of the drawing.
Something Rilke said comes to mind 'The *thing* is
definitive, the *art-thing* must be still more
definitive, removed from all accident...' (quite a
tall order from Rilke!) and Giacometti's struggle
with the drawing, which is carried out as much
with the rubber as the pencil, is his way of
conveying that struggle.

Alberto Giacometti, 1935

Do you remember the Giacometti exhibition at the Fundació Caixa Catalunya in Barcelona that we visited with Lali the morning after the *Cadmium Red* launch, when you spotted the quote about the colour grey? There is a famous series of photographs by Ernst Scheidegger in that catalogue showing the artist in his studio. One of the photos struck me (it's on the catalogue cover) because it seems to relate to the experience of looking directly into the face of one of his sculptures (there's a standing woman in the collection positioned close to Degas' *Little Dancer Aged 14*). Scheidegger's photograph is of a walking man sculpture in the making. The figure is striding forward with the same single-minded purpose that the portraits and standing sculptures have in their gaze and Giacometti appears to be seizing the moment to work on the hips as the figure passes him, adding more plaster before the walking man disappears out the door. It's as if once you step aside from that direct gaze you are invisible and the figure moves on.

A story in the collection catalogue tells how in 1949 Robert and Lisa Sainsbury bought two works by Giacometti from the Paris dealer, Pierre Loeb. The drawing I've been talking about, which cost them £6, and a painting of the artist's brother 'Diego Seated'. The painting from the previous year, wasn't signed and Loeb suggested going to the artist's studio and getting him to sign it.

Little Dancer, aged fourteen 1880/1

But, Robert Sainsbury remembers,
the dealer "warned us in the
strongest possible terms that we
mustn't take any notice when Giacometti
would probably tell us that the
painting, was not finished, and he
would like it back, because that would
be the end of it as far as we were
concerned. As you will understand
we had never met the said Alberto.
We went there and Pierre's forcast
was absolutely right, but we stood
firm: he signed it and we took it away."

Self portrait - oil - 1930

So far I have dwelt on the Giacometti drawing which
fascinates me but in this open room of screens,
directly to its left, is a self-portrait from 1930
by David Bomberg. A small, predominately brown
painting with a lighter V-shape denoting his shirt.
Again it is the eyes that intrigue you plus the
fact that the left side of his face is defined and
static while the right is blurred, almost as if it
has not quite stopped moving, and the right eye
has a smudge of paint across it rather like a
cataract.

'Lady in blue - oil - c/931

Bomberg and Giacometti face a painting from the 1930s by Soutine 'Lady in blue'. This is not one of my favourite pictures by him, I prefer those earlier, wilder works but perhaps I'm missing something in this case?

On the other side of the screen, with its back to the Soutine, is an interesting work by Bacon painted 1959 and acquired a year later, 'Two Figures in a Room', one of the small number of pieces in this collection that doesn't return your gaze. The figures in this picture don't avoid your look they are too involved in their own activity to be bothered whether we are watching or not.

Kneeling figure with attributes
of Osiris - Egypt c 1200 Bc

Two figures in a Room   1959

Statuette of a Striding man - Egypt - c. 2200 BC

Unlike the 20th-century works around them the
beautiful wooden and wax Egyptian figures placed
in their glass cases to left and right are sealed
in a ritual world of their own. They stare into
the far distance without any earthly questions on
their lips and seem to reaffirm the spiritual
division between the Egypt of 3 or 4000 years ago
and today. Then, as if to break this tidy
generalisation, just a few paces away the gaze of
the young boy in the Fayum mummy portrait catches
your eye and throws a spanner in the works. He's
alive and full of doubt and questions, like
Bomberg and Giacometti, and he's looking at you
across the 1900 or so years since he was painted.
He has a slightly sad and faraway look in his eye
which tells us perhaps that the artist who
painted him was contemplating his own mortality.

In this place you are surrounded by faces.

Statuette of a man - Egypt c2050 BC

mummy portrait of a youth - Egypt 100 AD

Dear John

I thought I would take you on a visit to a favourite place of mine, the Sainsbury Centre, on the outskirts of Norwich. It's a gallery I often visit, a wonderful mix of paintings, sculpture, drawings and objects collected over a lifetime by Robert and Lisa Sainsbury. I've made you this small book with gallery postcards and photos I took on my last visit to give you an idea of the place – I hope one day we will go there together.

The collection is housed in part of an elegantly detailed, hi-tech building designed by Norman Foster in 1973. It still looks good 40 years later.

There are always changing exhibitions but the highlight for me is the permanent collection and if we were walking in there now I would steer you, trying not to be distracted by any of the other works around us, through the series of spaces, created by free-standing screens. We would pass works by Bacon, Modigliani, Rouault, Picasso, Degas and Moore, as well as a wealth of Egyptian and Roman artefacts, masks and ritual objects from around the world to the picture that I always gravitate towards, Giacometti's self-portrait. I first saw this drawing in 1965 in his Tate retrospective. It was reproduced more or less full size on the cover of the catalogue. I found a note in the back of my copy giving the date I went to the show, 23rd August. When we moved to Suffolk in 2006 I found the drawing again, permanently on display and only about an hour's drive away.

You'd be aware too of the other works that surround you as you stand looking at the drawing; to the left a 1930s Bomberg self-portrait, behind you a rather restrained Soutine painting, *Lady in blue*, on either side of the Bomberg and Giacometti are some small wooden Egyptian figures, housed under glass, and behind you to the right, about 20 feet away, a Fayum mummy portrait of a young man from around AD100. So you are surrounded by eyes and perhaps it is the eyes that draw me to the Giacometti every time.

With just a pencil and a rubber, he has made an hypnotic image. I've looked hard at this drawing many times, standing the same distance from it that he stood when he drew it in 1935. I guess the mirror which he must have used to interrogate his face was probably slightly off to the left of his drawing board because he drew with his right hand. When you are looking at the drawing your eyes are where his eyes were.

Several things are striking and puzzling about this work. Although sections of it are undefined, because of the erasing, it has a very solid look to it, as though it's a drawing of a sculpted head. His wiry hair is a helmet, the ears just outline shapes, his left eye almost illegible, the remains of the drawing of his right eye stares directly at you. He gazes unblinking into the mirror at himself.

Inspecting the face close-up you notice the reference marks, either hard dots where his pencil lead rested or the short double strokes he placed at points over the surface; the neck, the hairline, the eye, the lips...etc. I tried covering up one side of the face and a curious thing happens. His right side fixes you with that slightly severe, direct look which is defined and emphasised by the down-turned mouth. His left side is more ambiguous, especially on the actual drawing rather than in a photo of it, because it can either look like the closed lid of a man asleep or the faint image of his open eye looking away from you to his left.

(I went back to the gallery this morning to look again at the drawing to see why I found this left eye – open/closed – so confused in my memory. On the actual drawing the eye is open and much less distinct than it appears on the postcard. I wondered why Giacometti didn't erase the eye altogether as he seemed well on the way to doing so – a few more strokes of the rubber would have done it. Then it dawned on me that this ambiguity creates a real tension and life in the drawing – the direct stare dominates the image but when you transfer your gaze to look at the other eye, expecting the same direct stare, Giacometti is looking away.)

I've watched footage of Giacometti talking and working (there's a good selection of clips on the internet) and he seems to have, in life, an open face with a faint smile about the lips. But it doesn't seem so in this drawing; here the face feels to me like a wall. It is the end of that 'narrow corridor of looking between you' which you describe, in your essay written just after he died in 1966. Perhaps it feels like an end because he is looking at a reflection of himself. It was also a self-portrait made in the year when he resumed modelling from nature after recently being excluded by Breton from the Surrealist group, a time when many friends, because of the split, distanced themselves from him.

Giacometti made these observations:

'One day when I was drawing a young girl, I suddenly noticed that the only thing that was alive was her gaze. The rest of her head meant no more to me than the skull of a dead man.'

'I knew that one day – no matter how it came about or what I was working towards, I would be forced to sit down on a stool before a model and copy what I saw. And with no hope of succeeding.'

Perhaps this anticipated failure before the object (even his own reflection) accounts for the erasing, or partial erasing, of areas of the drawing. Something Rilke said comes to mind 'The *thing* is definitive, the *art-thing* must be still more definitive, removed from all accident...' (quite a tall order from Rilke!) and Giacometti's struggle with the drawing, which is carried out as much with the rubber as the pencil, is his way of conveying that struggle.

Do you remember the Giacometti exhibition at the Fundació Caixa Catalunya in Barcelona that we visited with Lali (Bosch) the morning after the *Cadmium Red* launch, when you spotted the quote about the colour grey? There is a famous series of photo-graphs by Ernst Scheidegger in that catalogue showing the artist in his studio. One of the photos struck me (it's on the catalogue cover) because it seems to relate to the experience of looking directly into the face of one of his sculptures (there's a standing woman in the collection positioned close to Degas' *Little Dancer Aged 14*). Scheidegger's photograph is of a walking man sculpture in the making. The figure is striding forward with the same single-minded purpose that the portraits and standing sculptures have in their gaze and Giacometti appears to be seizing the moment to work on the hips as the figure passes him, adding more plaster before the walking man disappears out the door. It's as if once you step aside from that direct gaze you are invisible and the figure moves on.

A story in the collection catalogue tells how in 1949 Robert and Lisa Sainsbury bought two works by Giacometti from the Paris dealer, Pierre Loeb. The drawing I've been talking about, which cost them £6 and a painting of the artist's brother, *Diego Seated*. The painting, from the previous year, wasn't signed and Loeb suggested going to the painter's studio and getting him to sign it. But, Robert Sainsbury remembers, the dealer 'warned us in the strongest possible terms that we mustn't take any notice when Giacometti would probably tell us that the painting was not finished, and he would like it back, because that would be the end of it as far as we were concerned. As you will understand we had never met the said Alberto. We went there and Pierre's forecast was absolutely right, but we stood firm: he signed it and we took it away.'

So far I have dwelt on the Giacometti drawing which fascinates me but in this open room of screens, directly to its left, is a self-portrait from 1930 by David Bomberg. A small, predominately brown painting with a lighter V-shape denoting his shirt. Again it is the eyes that intrigue you plus the fact that the left side of his face is defined and static while the right is blurred, almost as if it has not quite stopped moving, and the right eye has a smudge of paint across it rather like a cataract.

Bomberg and Giacometti face Soutine's *Lady in blue*. This is not one of my favourite pictures by him, I prefer those earlier, wilder works but perhaps I'm missing something in this case?

On the other side of the screen, with its back to the Soutine, is an interesting work by Bacon painted 1959 and acquired a year later, *Two Figures in a Room,* one of the small number of pieces in this collection that doesn't return your gaze. The figures in this picture don't avoid your look they are too involved in their own activity to be bothered whether we are watching or not.

Unlike the 20th-century works around them the beautiful wooden and wax Egyptian figures placed in their glass cases to left and right are sealed in a ritual world of their own. They stare into the far distance without any earthly questions on their lips and seem to reaffirm the spiritual division between the Egypt of 3 or 4000 years ago and today. Then, as if to break this tidy generalisation, just a few paces away the gaze of the young boy in the Fayum mummy portrait catches your eye and throws a spanner in the works. He's alive and full of doubt and questions, like Bomberg and Giacometti, and he's looking at you across the 1900 years

since he was painted. He has a slightly sad and faraway look in his eye which tells us perhaps that the artist who painted him was contemplating his own mortality.

In this place you are surrounded by faces.

from John Berger February 2011

5/2/11.

John,

You take me for a walk through the Sainsbury Centre and you show me portraits — made sometime during the last two thousand years. Either painted or drawn. Why do we tend to exclude sculptures when we think of portraits? There have, after all, been many sculptured portraits. I think it's to do with the decapitation. The sculpted heads are dead still; whereas the painted and drawn ones are elusive and therefore alive. When a sculpted portrait includes a whole body — like Giacometti's Annette — there's no decapitation, and escape is still possible and therefore life is still elusive.

So you take me for a walk, and we look at portraits, and for me this is already intriguing for there is a special relationship between portraits and the act of walking, the acts of approaching, passing-by and leaving: A portrait is the creature of a confrontation, of a meeting. A kind of progeniture. Yet what remains, what hangs there on a wall afterwards, is not a presence but a trace. All portraits speak in a past tense. All sitters have walked on. Maybe thanks to the art of the twentieth century (Giacometti, Kokoshka, Auerbach) its easier for us to see and recognise this. But it was equally true at the time of Raphael or the Fayoum portraits. All portraits are traces which speak in a past tense.

This is why Scheidegger's photo of Giacometti in his studio is so apt. The sculpture of the striding man is every model, every sitter. He is on his way somewhere else. Like all sitters were. Alberto models him as he passes. He will never have time to finish him. And likewise all portraits, however smoothly "finished", however "polished", are unfinished. (What makes drawn portraits touching and intimate is that they don't disguise the fact that they are unfinished.)

Let's approach this from another angle — go behind another panel: A portrait is provisionally, but never definitively, finished by the spectator looking at it and taking it in. This is not the case for other categories of painting (landscapes, figures, objects, abstractions, myths); they are complete before the spectator arrives. Nor is it the case for photographic portraits because they have no beginning nor end; they are instantaneous. Every painted or drawn portrait is on its way somewhere else, a work prompted by departure. It temporarily arrives when recognised or identified by another, and then leaves again, seeking another arrival. Why is this? Portraits are nomad.

3.

Nomads, not in terms of space, but in terms
of time. Wandering between the past and the
future they reside in the present (they become
sedentary, as they were when they were
sitting for their ~~petered~~ portraits) only for so long
as they are being looked at. What confines
them to the present is another pair of eyes
meeting their own. When portraits are no
longer being looked at ⸢perhaps⸣ they shut their eyes?
~~they were~~ Are they ⸢like⸣ us when ~~we are~~ asleep?

I talk in riddles, because the aim
of portraits is itself a riddle, conjuring all
the while between absence and presence, solitude
and company. Portraits are a kind of
travel document. ~~But~~ At their best they
are not bureaucratic, but visionary.
Visionary visas.

Go to the National Portrait Gallery
and study the expressions of those
facing you. They of course vary. There
are, however, two main categories.
The retrospective one: "You don't know
where I have been and I can't tell you."
or the expectant one: "I'm looking
beyond ⸢you⸣ to where I'm going next."

4.

All this is a way of trying to approach your question about Giàcometti at his rubber. Which I'm going to come back to in my next letter.

My love to you all
John.

P.S.   I see a correspondence between portraits and abandoned garments. You come upon a shirt, a dress, a pair of gloves, a pair of shoes, left behind by somebody you know well. It is simultaneously the most intimate reminder of that person and a declaration of their absence. In the term likeness, isn't there already a feeling of loss?

Ikons are the opposite of portraits because their device ~~they are already~~ is to be surrounded by the eternal.

John

You take me for a walk through the Sainsbury Centre and you show me portraits – made sometime during the last two thousand years. Either painted or drawn. Why do we tend to exclude sculptures when we think of portraits? There have, after all, been many sculptured portraits. I think it is to do with the decapitation. The sculpted heads are dead still; whereas the painted and drawn ones are elusive and therefore alive. When a sculpted portrait includes a whole body – like Giacometti's *Annette* – there's no decapitation, and escape is still possible and therefore life is still elusive.

So you take me for a walk, and we look at portraits, and for me this is already intriguing for there is a special relationship between portraits and the act of walking, the acts of approaching, passing by and leaving. A portrait is the creature of a confrontation, a meeting. A kind of progeniture. Yet what remains, what hangs there on a wall afterwards, is not a presence but a trace. All portraits speak in a past tense. All sitters have walked on. Maybe thanks to the art of the twentieth century (Giacometti, Kokoschka, Auerbach) it's easier for us to see and recognise this. But it was equally true at the time of Raphael or the Fayoum portraits. All portraits are traces that speak in a past tense.

This is why Scheidegger's photo of Giacometti in his studio is so apt. The sculpture of the striding man is every model, every sitter. He is on his way somewhere else. Like all sitters were. Alberto models him as he passes. He will never have time to finish him. And likewise all portraits however smoothly 'finished', however 'polished', are unfinished. (What makes drawn portraits touching and intimate is that they don't disguise the fact that they are unfinished.)

Let's approach this from another angle – go behind another panel: a portrait is provisionally, but never definitively, finished by the spectator looking at it and taking it in. This is not the case for other categories of painting (landscapes, figures, objects, abstractions, myths); they are complete before the spectator arrives. Nor is it the case with photographic portraits because they have no beginning or end; they are instantaneous. Every painted or drawn portrait is on its way somewhere else, a work prompted by departure. It temporarily arrives when recognised or identified by another, and then leaves again, seeking another arrival. Why is this? Portraits are nomad. Nomads, not in terms of space, but in terms of time. Wandering between the past and the future they reside in the present (they become sedentary, as they were when they were sitting for their portraits) only for so long as they are being looked at. What confines them to the present is another pair of eyes meeting their own. When portraits are no longer being looked at perhaps they shut their eyes? Are they like us when asleep?

I talk in riddles because the aim of portraits is itself a riddle, conjuring all the while between absence and presence, solitude and company. Portraits are a kind of travel document. At their best they are not bureaucratic, but visionary. Visionary visas.
Go to the National Portrait Gallery and study the expressions of those facing you. They of course vary. There are, however, two main categories. The retrospective one: 'You don't know where I have been and I can't tell you' or the expectant one: 'I am looking beyond you to where I'm going next.'

All this is a way of trying to approach your question of Giacometti and his rubber. Which I am going to come back to in my next letter.
My love to you all
John

P.S. I see a correspondence between portraits and abandoned garments. You come upon a shirt, a dress, a pair of gloves, a pair of shoes, left behind by somebody you know well. It is simultaneously the most intimate reminder of that person and a declaration of their absence. In the term likeness, isn't there already a feeling of loss?

Ikons are the opposite of portraits because their device is to be surrounded by the eternal.

from John Christie March 2011

On his way somewhere else

Dear John   18/3/11

I visited Norwich again today but this time,
instead of heading to my usual starting place in
front of Giacometti, I was looking for an unfamiliar
drawing. Something in your letter, the mention of
portraits speaking in a past tense and the example
of Giacometti, Kokoschka and Auerbach made me
want to search for Auerbach's *Portrait of Leon
Kossoff* in the collection.

It is not in the main display on the ground floor
so I headed to the reserve collection which is on
the lower level, below ground in a new extension
added in 1991. You descend a spiral staircase,
just inside the main entrance, walk through the
bookshop and along the corridor with education
studios and displays on either side. At the end
there is a row of windows which break the ground
and let in daylight. To the right is another
temporary exhibition gallery and you pass through
the reserve collection to get to it. This reserve
collection is not hidden away (apart from the
underground walk to get to it) as in most major
museums where special permission is needed to see
the works. Here the things are quite tightly hung
in display cabinets, but all on view.

Just round to the left, as I entered, was the
Auerbach portrait. I'd seen a reproduction of it
in the catalogue but it was bigger (66 x 53cms)
than I'd imagined, the heavy head, which is looking
down, is almost life-sized. So here we have a
face, unlike the Giacometti, averting it's gaze.
The dense black charcoal is worked hard and in
places the paper has been rubbed away and patched
up. It feels like damage from a prolonged and
concerted scuffle.

Portrait of Leon Kossoff   Frank Auerbach '57

When I got home I looked through my books and found two on Auerbach; a catalogue from his 1978 Hayward show and an interesting monograph by Robert Hughes in which the artist describes his working method:'...the way I work means putting up a whole image, and dismantling it and putting up another whole image, which is...physically extremely strenuous...'

There are also in the book a series of 40 photographs of the progress of a drawing he did of Kitaj's wife, Sandra Fisher. One picture taken at the end of each session where the image and position of her face alters on the paper in the way he describes above. So that the drawing each time builds on what is left from the session before – the original white paper only glimpsed when the eraser cuts through the layers of charcoal – the drawing built on this accumulation of dust becomes again only the physical work of that particular day – all the previous efforts hidden, like an iceberg, beneath its surface.

Auerbach did a portrait drawing of Robert Hughes, possibly during the time he was interviewing him for the book, where Hughes observes another interesting aspect of the making of the drawing:

'....Now and again he (Auerbach) fumbles out a book from a nearby shelf, opens it to a reproduction – Giacometti's *Woman with her Throat Cut*, Cézanne's *Self-portrait with Cap*, from the Hermitage, Vermeer's young turbaned girl – and lays it on the floor where he can see it, "to have something good to look at", a purpose not kind to the sitter's vanity until one understands that Auerbach is hoping for osmosis.'

Studying the *Portrait of Leon Kossoff*, looking

down and seemingly deep in the mystery of his own thoughts, I remembered a funny story concerning the interpretation of expression in a portrait.

When I was making a documentary for Channel Four in the early 90s about the Soho photographer John Deakin I came across a portrait of him by Lucian Freud that I wanted to use in the film. The painting, which evidently took months to complete, shows Deakin, full-face, gazing slightly down with a melancholy look about him. A look that seemed to perfectly capture the character of this strange, difficult man who didn't value the photographic work that he is now remembered for but longed to be a painter like his drinking friends Bacon and Freud.

It turned out that this lost look can be explained by a number of other factors. Deakin was collected early each morning, perhaps still suffering from the previous night's hang-over, by Freud in his sports car and driven at speed to the studio (Caroline Blackwood said, 'If you've ever been driven by Lucian you'll know exactly what it was like being married to him!'). Once there he was plied with retsina to quieten him down while the work got under way. One lunchtime, after many weeks of sittings for Freud, Deakin dashed into the French House in Dean Street, and announced in despair, 'Lucian's unhappy with the portrait, he's scraped it all off, we're starting again.'

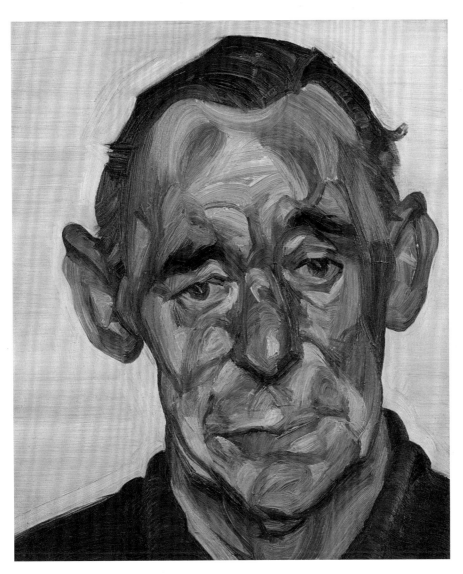

John Deakin   Lucian Freud 1964

Interestingly, and it didn't strike me immediately
as I was distracted by the worn, worked surface
of Auerbach's drawing but suddenly it seemed to
me that in the portrait Kossoff, whatever he had
on his mind, appeared to be walking away. Or, if
he was sitting down, to be on the point of standing
and moving off. His weight is forward towards the
left and the dynamic lines, where the white
eraser marks have sliced through to the paper,
suggest movement in the same direction – an example
perhaps of what you talked about in your last
letter, of a work being 'on its way somewhere
else'. You might feel you want to stop him before
he goes – but, (is it too fanciful to feel this?)
he's not interested or is indifferent to the
viewer's attention?
With the Giacometti, and other portraits which
look directly out of the picture, it is they who
engage us on their own terms. We can look away
but we know they are still staring at us. Whereas
we cannot engage the Auerbach through eye
contact, Leon Kossoff, in the portrait, is not
concerned with us and we get not a glance from
him. It is as though we are looking through a
window and unable to attract his attention.

Between people it is possible to "catch
someone's eye" – it happens sometimes
when you are in a car or bus travelling
along a busy street that there can be
a sudden direct eye connection between
you and a stranger, even at a good
distance, just an unexplained,
momentary and mostly unwanted connection.
Then you've both moved on and it's broken.
A bit like snagging your sleeve on a
sharp corner which temporarily stops you
but, once unhooked, you move on.

Back upstairs I went onto the mezzanine above the main gallery to look at Giacometti's bust of *Annette without Arms* and found close-by a perfect example of what you describe as 'decapitation', a beautiful Roman portrait bust from the first century AD. Although it is under glass the head makes you want to stroke the surface of the marble to feel its perfection and coolness. But the eyes are blank, the eyes of a blind man, and the face is passive – it fits your description of sculpted heads being 'dead still'.

Roman Portrait Head   c. AD 1-50

The bust of Annette, unlike Giacometti's full-length standing figure on the floor below, has no arms or legs, a portrait head on a rudimentary torso, but she is very much alive and in her own space unlike her Roman neighbour. When I moved directly in front of her face one chameleon-like eye, her left, fixed me with a direct hard stare whilst the other looked over my shoulder to something happening behind me. It is the same device Giacometti employs in his self-portrait drawing and has the effect of animating the face and also introducing the element of time into the portrait. As you look from eye to eye and the direction of gaze changes you feel as though time has been stretched or there has been a 'jump' in time. In the catalogue entry concerning this work it describes how Giacometti told the Sainsburys that he preferred to model the back of the head while continuing to face it from the front.

It is not surprising to find this is
the case considering his statement
which I sent you last time:
"... the only thing that was alive
was her gaze. The rest of her
head meant no more to me than
the skull of a dead man."

Ossip Zadkine — bronze 1918

Finally, here are a couple of photos showing a small sculpture by Zadkine which I was drawn to on the way out. It is surrounded by a circle of eyes. Works by Modigliani, Bacon and a standing nude drawing by Giacometti gaze at The Accordion Player who seems to be lost in his own music. I would have liked to have taken him home with me for a day or two.

I'm looking forward to hearing your thoughts on Giacometti's self portrait drawing.
I almost called him Alberto —
I've been spending quite a bit of time with him lately.

With Love from us all.

John.

Dear John

I visited Norwich again today but this time, instead of heading to
my usual starting place in front of Giacometti, I was looking for
an unfamiliar drawing. Something in your letter, the mention of
portraits speaking in a past tense and the example of Giacometti,
Kokoschka and Auerbach made me want to search for Auerbach's
Portrait of Leon Kossoff in the collection. It is not in the main display
on the ground floor so I headed to the reserve collection which
is on the lower level, below ground in a new extension added in
1991. You descend a spiral staircase, just inside the main entrance,
walk through the bookshop and along the corridor with education
studios and displays on either side. At the end there is a row of
windows which break the ground and let in daylight. To the right
is another temporary exhibition gallery and you pass through the
reserve collection to get to it. This reserve collection is not hidden
away (apart from the underground walk to get to it) as in most
major museums where special permission is needed to see the
works. Here the things are quite tightly hung in display cabinets,
but all on view. Just round to the left, as I entered, was the Auerbach
portrait. I'd seen a reproduction of it in the catalogue but it was
bigger (66 x 53cms) than I'd imagined, the heavy head, which is
looking down, is almost life-sized. So here we have a face, unlike
the Giacometti, averting it's gaze. The dense black charcoal is
worked hard and in places the paper has been rubbed away and
patched up. It feels like damage from a prolonged and concerted
scuffle.

When I got home I looked through my books and found two
on Auerbach; a catalogue from his 1978 Hayward show and an
interesting monograph by Robert Hughes in which the artist
describes his working method:

'...the way I work means putting up a whole image, and dismantling
it and putting up another whole image, which is ...physically
extremely strenuous...'

There are also in the book a series of 40 photographs of the
progress of a drawing he did of Kitaj's wife, Sandra Fisher. One
picture taken at the end of each session where the image and
position of her face alters on the paper in the way he describes
above. So that the drawing each time builds on what is left from
the session before – the original white paper only glimpsed when
the eraser cuts through the layers of charcoal – the drawing built
on this accumulation of dust becomes again only the physical
work of that particular day – all the previous efforts hidden, like
an iceberg, beneath its surface.

Auerbach did a portrait drawing of Robert Hughes, possibly during
the time he was interviewing him for the book, where Hughes
observes another interesting aspect of the making of the drawing:

'....Now and again he (Auerbach) fumbles out a book from a
nearby shelf, opens it to a reproduction – Giacometti's *Woman
with her Throat Cut,* Cézanne's *Self-portrait with Cap,* from the
Hermitage, Vermeer's young turbaned girl – and lays it on the
floor where he can see it, "to have something good to look at"

a purpose not kind to the sitter's vanity until one understands that Auerbach is hoping for osmosis.'

Studying the *Portrait of Leon Kossoff*, looking down and seemingly deep in the mystery of his own thoughts, I remembered a funny story concerning the interpretation of expression in a portrait.

When I was making a documentary for Channel Four in the early 90s about the Soho photographer John Deakin I came across a portrait (unfortunately not in the Sainsbury collection) of him by Lucian Freud that I wanted to use in the film. The painting, which evidently took months to complete, shows Deakin, full-face, gazing slightly down with a melancholy look about him. A look that seemed to perfectly capture the character of this strange, difficult man who didn't value the photographic work that he is now remembered for but longed to be a painter like his drinking friends Bacon and Freud. It turned out that this lost look can be explained by a number of other factors. Deakin was collected early each morning, perhaps still suffering from the previous night's hang-over, by Freud in his sports car and driven at speed to the studio (Caroline Blackwood said, 'If you've ever been driven by Lucian you'll know exactly what it was like being married to him!'). Once there he was plied with retsina to quieten him down while the work got under way. One lunchtime, after many weeks of sittings for Freud, Deakin dashed into the French House in Dean Street and announced in despair, 'Lucian's unhappy with the portrait, he's scraped it all off, we're starting again.'

Interestingly, and it didn't strike me immediately as I was distracted by the worn, worked surface of Auerbach's drawing but suddenly it seemed on me that in the portrait Kossoff, whatever he had on his mind, appeared to be walking away. Or, if he was sitting down, to be on the point of standing and moving off. His weight is forward towards the left and the dynamic lines, where the white eraser marks have sliced through to the paper, suggest movement in the same direction – an example perhaps of what you talked about in your last letter, of a work being 'on its way somewhere else'. You might feel you want to stop him before he goes – but, (is it too fanciful to feel this?) he's not interested or is indifferent to the viewer's attention?

With the Giacometti, and other portraits which look directly out of the picture, it is they who engage us on their own terms. We can look away but we know they are still staring at us. Whereas we cannot engage the Auerbach through eye contact, Leon Kossoff, in the portrait, is not concerned with us and we get not a glance from him. It is as though we are looking through a window and unable to attract his attention.

Between people it is possible to 'catch someone's eye' – it happens sometimes when you are in a car or bus travelling along a busy street, that there can be a sudden direct eye connection between you and a stranger, even at a good distance, just an unexplained, momentary and mostly unwanted connection. Then you've both moved on and the thread is broken. A bit like snagging your sleeve on a sharp corner which temporarily stops you but, once unhooked, you move on.

Back upstairs I went onto the mezzanine above the main gallery to look at Giacometti's bust of *Annette without Arms* and found close-by a perfect example of what you describe as 'decapitation', a beautiful Roman portrait bust from the first century AD. Although it is under glass the head makes you want to stroke the surface of the marble to feel its perfection and coolness. But the eyes are blank, the eyes of a blind man, and the face is passive – it fits your description of sculpted heads being 'dead still'.

The bust of Annette, unlike Giacometti's full-length standing figure on the floor below, has no arms or legs, a portrait head on a rudimentary torso, but she is very much alive and in her own space unlike her Roman neighbour. When I moved directly in front of her face one chameleon-like eye, her left, fixed me with a direct hard stare whilst the other looked over my shoulder to something happening behind me. It is the same device Giacometti employs in his self-portrait drawing and has the effect of animating the face and also introducing the element of time into the portrait. As you look from eye to eye and the direction of gaze changes you feel as though time has been stretched or there has been a 'jump' in time.

In the catalogue entry concerning this work it describes how Giacometti told the Sainsburys that he preferred to model the back of the head while continuing to face it from the front.

It is not surprising to find this was the case considering his statement which I sent you last time,
'...the only thing that was alive was her gaze. The rest of her head meant no more to me than the skull of a dead man.'

Finally here are a couple of photos of a small sculpture by Zadkine which I was drawn to on the way out. It is surrounded by a circle of eyes. Works by Modigliani, Bacon and a standing nude drawing by Giacometti gaze at *The Accordion Player* who seems to be lost in his own music. I would have liked to have taken him home with me for a day or two.

I'm looking forward to hearing your thoughts on Giacometti's self-portrait drawing. I almost called him Alberto – I've been spending quite a bit of time with him lately.

With love from us all
John

from John Berger April 2011

John,

Thank you for the chapter "Surrounded by Faces", and the portrait of L.K. You are right — he too is on the point of leaving. And, as you say, he's ignoring us; we can't attract his attention. Yet it seems to me something surprising happens as a consequence of this. It doesn't make him more remote, because we identify with him, a kind of ~~osmosis takes place~~, we imagine holding our head as he holds his, we ~~sense the~~ light falling on our forehead as it falls on his. We, too, are about to get up and move forward. ~~but~~. ~~And~~ This would not occur if there was an eye contact between us.

On the next page where you show a close-up detail of Kossof's head, it becomes clearer that the drama of this drawing has little to do with his character or his story ~~or his story~~ but a lot to do with the drama of a solid thing (his head) occupying space. It's about the mystery of space. Or, as Spinoza would put it, about the mystery of extension.

2.

"The object of the idea constituting the human mind is the body, or a certain mode of extension actually existing and nothing else" (Prop. XIII. Pt 2. Ethics)

On the following page there's Freud's portrait of John Deakin which is very different. It is only concerned with character: the character of the sitter and the character of the painterly representation. It's very close to caricature and no mystery of existential space exists here. Auerbach's drawing of Kossof is like a note scribbled, erased, worked on again by an astronomer; and Freud's painting by contrast is like gossip.

The mystery of space occupying space is philosophically inseperable from the riddle or mystery, of occupying time. And it's with this thought that we can now return to Alberto's self-portrait of 1935.

His use of the rubber is intimiately connected with time. Time which rubs us out. Of course he applied the rubber because he saw an error which he wanted to correct, not because he was pondering time:

Yet he usually stopped before everything was erased. Why? Because he wanted visible traces of the erasures. They suggested a process which he wanted the drawing to contain and include. And in that process there was the passing of time, the ~~inevitability~~ inevitibility of change. A drawing like this is the opposite of a photograph which seizes the definitive moment and stops time. In this drawing time is as much there as the features of his face as he looks into the mirror. The quicksilver of a life...

What is so extraordinary about Alberto is his ~~reticence~~ mixture of persistance and reticence. His stance towards what he is producing — whether drawing, painting or sculpture — is like that of a mountaineer towards a mountain he is climbing. The mountain climbed becomes his achievement and he has no need or desire for any other attention.

Bonnard's self-portrait, as you point out, is in some ways similar to Alberto's, a similar disparity between the two eyes. But the great difference is in the character of the marks, ~~the traces~~ of the gestures of the hand holding a paint-brush or pencil on the canvas or paper. Bonnard's gestures are flourishes; he wants them to be noticed for themselves. Alberto's are like traces of something inadvertantly left behind.

4 .

Like a footprint. He believed that the essence of what was in front of him — whether his own head or annette's body — had to be <u>made</u> to appear. It was not a given. And the act of appearing, if it happens, is almost indistinguishable from the act of disappearing. When we come upon a revelation, is it something which is coming, or which is going?

Maybe I can put this in a clearer way. Giacometti's figures — whether drawn or cast — represent not the Being of a person but the Becoming of a person. Hence their premonition of choice and Freedom. And hence too, their familiarity with doubt.

The Zadkine makes me happy. The way he sculpts the accordian, is a bit like the two words: Sing-Song. He was a tiny man (in physical size) and he had a very Russian sense of music. What does that mean? For them the musical impulse — not necessarily the form — is choral. It unites people.

Love
John

John

Thank you for the portrait of L.K. You are right – he too is on the point of leaving. And, as you say, he's ignoring us; we can't attract his attention. Yet it seems to me that something surprising happens as a consequence of this. It doesn't make him more remote, because we identify with him, we imagine holding our head as he holds his, we sense the light falling on our forehead as it falls on his. We, too, are about to get up and move forward. This would not occur if there was eye contact between us.

On the next page where you show a close-up of Kossoff's head, it becomes clearer that the drama of this drawing has little to do with his character or his story but a lot to do with the drama of a solid thing (his head) occupying space. It's the mystery of space. Or, as Spinoza would put it, about the mystery of extension.

'The object of the idea constituting the human mind is the body, or a certain mode of extension actually existing and nothing else.' [Ethics. Prop. XIII. Pt.2]

On the following page there's Freud's portrait of John Deakin which is very different. It is only concerned with character: the character of the sitter and the character of the painterly representation. It's very close to caricature, and no mystery of existential space exists here. Auerbach's drawing of Kossoff is like a note scribbled, erased, worked on again by an astronomer; and Freud's painting by contrast is like gossip.

The mystery of occupying space is philosophically inseparable from the riddle, or mystery, of occupying time. And it's with this thought that we can now return to Alberto's self-portrait of 1935.

His use of the rubber is intimately connected with time. Time which rubs us out. Of course he applied the rubber because he saw an error which he wanted to correct, not because he was pondering time. Yet he usually stopped before everything was erased. Why? Because he wanted visible traces of the erasures. They suggested a process that he wanted the drawing to contain and include. And in that process there was the passing of time, the inevitability of change. A drawing like this is the opposite of a photograph which seizes 'the definitive moment' and stops time. In this drawing time is as much there as the features of his face as he looks into the mirror. The quicksilver of life ...

What is so extraordinary about Alberto is his mixture of persistence and reticence. His stance towards what he is producing – whether drawing, painting or sculpture – is like that of a mountaineer towards a mountain he is climbing. The mountain climbed becomes his achievement, and he has no need or desire for any other attention.

Bomberg's portrait, as you point out, is in some ways similar to Alberto's, a similar disparity between the two eyes. But the great difference is in the character of the marks, the gestures of the hand holding a paintbrush or pencil on the canvas or paper.

Bomberg's gestures are flourishes; he wants them to be noticed for themselves. Alberto's are like traces of something inadvertently left behind. Like a footprint. He believed that the essence of what was in front of him – whether his own head or Annette's body – had to be made to appear. It was not a given. And the act of appearing, if it happens, is almost indistinguishable from the act of disappearing. When we come upon a revelation, is it something which is coming, or which is going?

Maybe I can put it a clearer way. Giacometti's figures – whether drawn or cast – represent not the Being of a person but the Becoming of a person. Hence their premonition of Choice and Freedom. And hence, too, their familiarity with doubt.

The Zadkine makes me happy. The way he sculpts the accordion is a bit like the two words Sing–Song! He was a tiny man (in physical size) and he had a very Russian sense of music. What does that mean? For them the musical impulse – not necessarily the form – is choral. It unites people.

Love John

from John Christie May 2011

A small gesture

Dear John   11. May 2011

I made a trip to the gallery on Saturday and this
time Alice came with me. I wanted to talk through
with her some of the ideas that you and I have
been discussing but works had been changed around
a little and the portrait of L.K. wasn't there.
Maybe he'd managed to make off at last leaving
just charcoal dust behind. But the Zadkine
Accordionist was still on the plinth where I'd
left him, swaying to his music. I looked in a
reference book for an image of his powerful
monument *The Destroyed City* which I've only ever
seen in photos. I'm sure you must have seen it in
Rotterdam, perhaps when it was first erected? Did
you ever meet Zadkine? You say in your letter 'he
was a tiny man' so probably you did. It is
interesting that the man who made the small-scale
Accordionist, a sculpture that produces feelings of
happiness, could also have in his gut the anger
and strength to produce that image of defiance
coupled with terror in Rotterdam. It's powerful
and universal enough to be sited in any bombed
city in the world.

I've been thinking about the two categories of
portrait drawings that we've been discussing, the
portrait that gazes back (as in the Giacometti)
and the portrait (the Auerbach drawing of L.K.)
where, either coming or going, the subject is
indifferent to the viewer. Into this second
category, I think, come works where the dividing
line is blurred between portrait and still life.

In the collection there is a beautiful drawing by
Giacometti of a skull, the earliest work they have
of his, which seems to me to be a demonstration of
that dividing line or frontier. The drawing was
made in 1923 when Giacometti was a student studying

in Paris under the sculptor Antoine Bourdelle and
the skull has the appearance of facetted stone –
literally like a rock face.

Giacometti wouldn't have known the person whose
skull he was drawing, it was probably part of the
Académy's box of props, but the way he has drawn it
(there's a strong feeling of Cézanne about it) has
somehow brought life back to the bone and makes us
conscious that once this was a living, breathing
person, perhaps somebody's father or mother?
Giacometti has heavily worked the face area but has
left the rest of the skull, the container of lost
memories, thoughts and emotions, as a barely
indicated shell.

If we move the dividing line back from Giacometti's unnamed skull/portrait towards the portraits of the living along the way we come to drawings of the dead or dying. Here, I have to say, because I've never made a drawing of a dead person, I'm in the dark. I was going to say *never had to make* – as there seems an element of compulsion and urgency about the need to do it – but I know you have and have written about the experience too. I remember that drawing of your father above your work table and the moving account of making the drawing of him in his coffin. As you say in your essay, 'What you are drawing will never be seen again, by you or by anybody else. In the whole course of time past and time to come, this moment is unique: the last opportunity to draw what will never again be visible, which has occurred once and will never reoccur.'

I remember Jean saying during the making of *Another Way of Telling*, after he photographed the 84-years-old Marcel for our film, that he thought there was a time when old people should be left in peace, not photographed, and that Marcel had passed that point. I recall him also talking about the dilemma of taking pictures of blind people or people who were asleep and unaware of what you are doing – I think he was worrying about permission, taking something without permission. Of course it is easier to take, without permission, a photograph in a split second than it is to draw someone because of the element of time involved. When you reach the point of drawing someone who is dying, or has died, then I suppose you are the one who has to supply your own permission.

Maggi Hambling 'father' 18.1.98

Maggi did a very powerful series of drawings in
1998 of her father, Harry Hambling, as he lay
dying in an Ipswich hospital and, after his death,
in the chapel of rest. Her drawings too, done over
a period of 17 days, contain that need to look and
keep looking at a face that would soon disappear.
I don't think it is the urgency of her line as it
builds the likeness on the paper but what comes
through is the intensity of her looking, the
constant striving at one more attempt, while there
is time, before the face goes forever.

Harry Hambling was 95 when he died and from Maggi's
drawings you can see he was a very old man.
Your father doesn't look very old in your drawing
although I remember he had served in the First
World War so was probably at least in his mid-70s?

My dad died in 1964 when he was 49. I was 19 at
the time. He died on the day he was due to come
home from hospital after six weeks' convalescence.
I don't think I'd been to see him during that
time because the convalescence home was some
distance away at Banstead, south of London, and
there was no feeling of urgency, we knew he'd be
back home soon. With my mum, sister and brother
I'd helped decorate the house while he'd been
away and a hire-purchase agreement had been
signed to buy a new settee and armchairs for the
front room. This was an unusual move for my mum
because she comes from that generation who always
insist on paying their way, who would rather do
without if they can't afford something. Buying
that furniture on the 'never-never' was another
indication that none of us saw what was coming.

At 8am a policeman called at our house in the
East End – we didn't have a telephone – to say
that there was a problem at the hospital, my dad
had had a heart attack while washing and shaving
in readiness for the journey home and the doctors
thought we should come immediately.

I went with my mum to Banstead. It was an awkward
journey with a few changes of train along the way
and we didn't get there until about noon. My dad
was in bed in a room on his own, he had tubes in
his nose and arm. He was going in and out of
consciousness but knew we were there and perhaps
even briefly spoke, I can't remember.

I must say I felt completely helpless sitting there by his bedside and just wanted to get away from that room. After a while I told my mum that I was going home to get my motor bike and I'd be back later.

When I eventually returned I walked back through the empty corridors. The door of his room was closed and I could hear voices chatting and activity inside. Something, probably the different sounds coming from behind the door, told me that things had changed inside the room and I turned and walked away without going in.

I found my mum sitting on a bench in a side corridor, she was in tears and told me dad had died a little while before. I was only a learner rider at the time and not supposed to take passengers but I drove her away from the hospital on the back of the bike. The new furniture was returned the following week after the funeral.

The memory from that day, the last sight I'd seen of my dad, in that hospital bed, had made me want to escape and by escaping I'd lost the chance of seeing him again. I've been wondering if I could have sat down and drawn a portrait of him as you did with your father and Maggi with hers but I know I couldn't have. It's not about whether I had the skill to do a drawing – I remember you saying once that if you need to make a drawing you'll find a way to do it – no, I don't think I had the courage. I hadn't had the courage to stay at the hospital with my mum and making a drawing would have been an acknowledgement, a proof if you like if proof were needed, that his death had happened, and I chose not to face up to it at that moment.

I have family photographs of course, in lieu of a drawing, and here is one I found recently. It's a picture taken in the '50s by a professional photographer outside the fish and poultry shop that my dad managed in South Kensington, opposite Harrods. He is wearing his white shop coat, holding a pencil in his right hand and his order book, like a badge of office, in the other and you can just see a sales blackboard propped up in the doorway announcing: *Special – English Rabbits*. It looks as though he was working when the photographer asked him to step outside the shop onto the pavement of Brompton Road for the picture. I'm not sure why the photo was taken but it reminds me of those formal portraits of German society from the 1920s in August Sander's *People of the 20th Century*.

I have no idea who the slightly sinister-looking character is in the background, with his double-breasted suit and pocket handkerchief, he looks as though he has stepped straight out of a gangster film (who or what he was we'll never know). Perhaps it's his gaze and the cigarette smoke crossing the lower part of his face, or his black suit in contrast to my dad's white coat, that draws your eye to him, what is certain is that he has his own story which is lost to us. I'm sure if Sander had been taking the picture he would have told him to leave the frame.

I remember going with my dad several times when I was quite young, probably 10 or 12 years old, to Billingsgate. At four in the morning the whole market was alive and as we went round everyone seemed to know him. An odd thing for me was that, although his name was Bill, all the traders called him Mr Chris or Chris, an affectionate shortening of his surname.

In Alex Danchev's *George Braque, A Life* I found this: 'Giacometti was prevailed upon to continue an ancient tradition and to make a drawing of Braque on his deathbed. In the still of the morning after (as it happened a Sunday), with Jean Leymarie in attendance for moral support, he struggled for several hours to discharge his responsibility to his satisfaction...Giacometti considered the result a failure. It was as if his subject refused to give up the ghost. "Each time I finished a drawing it was a living Braque. Curious, no?"'

At the end of your essay about the drawing of your father you say, "from being a site of departure, it has become a site of arrival. Every day more of my father's life returns to the drawing in front of me."

I don't have a drawing as a magnet to attract memories but I do have this small gesture.
When I was growing up I used to watch my dad shaving, probably all boys do. To begin to shave means you are turning into a man. I watched him indirectly but carefully, to learn the tricks of the trade, as it were, and one of the things he always did after putting the shaving soap on his face was to use the knuckle of the first finger on his right hand and draw it across his lips, from left to right, to clear the soap. I still do that each time I shave and every time I think of him.
                    With love from us all
                                John.

Dear John

I made a trip to the gallery on Saturday and this time Alice came with me. I wanted to talk through with her some of the ideas that you and I have been discussing but works had been changed around a little and the portrait of L.K. wasn't there, maybe he'd managed to make off at last leaving just charcoal dust behind. But the Zadkine *Accordionist* was still on the plinth where I'd left him, swaying to his music. I looked in a reference book for an image of his powerful monument *The Destroyed City* which I've only ever seen in photos. I'm sure you must have seen it in Rotterdam, perhaps when it was first erected? Did you ever meet Zadkine? You say in your letter 'he was a tiny man' so probably you did. It is interesting that the man who made the small-scale *Accordionist*, a sculpture that produces feelings of happiness, could also have in his gut the anger and strength to produce that image of defiance coupled with terror in Rotterdam. It's powerful and universal enough to be sited in any bombed city in the world.

I've been thinking about the two categories of portrait drawings that we've been discussing, the portrait that gazes back (as in the Giacometti) and the portrait (the Auerbach drawing of L.K.) where, either coming or going, the subject is indifferent to the viewer. Into this second category, I think, come works where the dividing line is blurred between portrait and still life. In the collection there is a beautiful drawing by Giacometti of a skull, the earliest work they have of his, which seems to me to be a demonstration of that dividing line or frontier. The drawing was made in 1923 when Giacometti was a student studying in Paris under the sculptor Antoine Bourdelle and the skull has the appearance of facetted stone – literally like a rock face.

Giacometti wouldn't have known the person whose skull he was drawing, it was probably part of the Académy's box of props, but the way he has drawn it (there's a strong feeling of Cézanne about it) has somehow brought life back to the bone and makes us conscious that once this was a living, breathing person, perhaps somebody's father or mother? Giacometti has heavily worked the face area but has left the rest of the skull, the container of lost memories, thoughts and emotions, as a barely indicated shell.

If we move the dividing line back from Giacometti's unnamed skull/portrait towards the portraits of the living along the way we come to drawings of the dead or dying. Here, I have to say, because I've never made a drawing of a dead person, I'm in the dark. I was going to say *never had to make* – as there seems an element of compulsion and urgency about the need to do it – but I know you have and have written about the experience too. I remember that drawing of your father above your work table and the moving account of making the drawing of him in his coffin. As you say in your essay, 'What you are drawing will never be seen again, by you or by anybody else. In the whole course of time past and time to come, this moment is unique: the last opportunity to draw what will never again be visible, which has occurred once and will never reoccur.'

I remember Jean (Mohr) saying during the making of *Another Way*

of Telling, after he photographed the 84-years-old Marcel for our film, that he thought there was a time when old people should be left in peace, not photographed, and that Marcel had passed that point. I recall him also talking about the dilemma of taking pictures of blind people or people who were asleep and unaware of what you are doing – I think he was worrying about permission, taking something without permission. Of course it is easier to take, without permission, a photograph in a split-second than it is to draw someone because of the element of time involved. When you reach the point of drawing someone who is dying, or has died, then I suppose you are the one who has to supply your own permission.

Maggi (Hambling) did a very powerful series of drawings in 1998 of her father, Harry Hambling, as he lay dying in an Ipswich hospital and, after his death, in the chapel of rest. Her drawings too, done over a period of 17 days, contain that need to look and keep looking at a face that would soon disappear. I don't think it is the urgency of her line as it builds the likeness on the paper but what comes through is the intensity of her looking, the constant striving at one more attempt, while there is time, before the face goes forever.

Harry Hambling was 95 when he died and from Maggi's drawings you can see he was a very old man. Your father doesn't look very old in your drawing although I remember he had served in the First World War so was probably at least in his mid-70s?

My dad died in 1964 when he was 49. I was 19 at the time. He died on the day he was due to come home from hospital after six weeks convalescence. I don't think I'd been to see him during that time because the convalescence home was some distance away at Banstead, south of London, and there was no feeling of urgency, we knew he'd be back home soon. With my mum, sister and brother I'd helped decorate the house while he'd been away and a hire-purchase agreement had been signed to buy a new settee and armchairs for the front room. This was an unusual move for my mum because she comes from that generation who always insist on paying their way, who would rather do without if they can't afford something. Buying that furniture on the 'never-never' was another indication that none of us saw what was coming.

At 8am a policeman called at our house in the East End – we didn't have a telephone – to say that there was a problem at the hospital, my dad had had a heart attack while washing and shaving in readiness for the journey home and the doctors thought we should come immediately.

I went with my mum to Banstead. It was an awkward journey with a few changes of train along the way and we didn't get there until about noon. My dad was in bed in a room on his own, he had tubes in his nose and arm. He was going in and out of consciousness but knew we were there and perhaps even briefly spoke, I can't remember.

I must say I felt completely helpless sitting there by his bedside and just wanted to get away from that room. After a while I told my mum that I was going home to get my motor bike and I'd be back later.

When I eventually returned I walked back through the empty corridors. The door of his room was closed and I could hear voices chatting and activity inside. Something, probably the different sounds coming from behind the door, told me that things had changed inside the room and I turned and walked away without going in.

I found my mum sitting on a bench in a side corridor, she was in tears and told me dad had died a little while before. I was only a learner rider at the time and not supposed to take passengers but I drove her away from the hospital on the back of the bike. The new furniture was returned the following week after the funeral.

The memory from that day, the last sight I'd seen of my dad, in that hospital bed, had made me want to escape and by escaping I'd lost the chance of seeing him again. I've been wondering if I could have sat down and drawn a portrait of him as you did with your father and Maggi with hers but I know I couldn't have. It's not about whether I had the skill to do a drawing – I remember you saying once that if you need to make a drawing you'll find a way to do it – no, I don't think I had the courage. I hadn't had the courage to stay at the hospital with my mum and making a drawing would have been an acknowledgement, a proof if you like if proof were needed, that his death had happened, and I chose not to face up to it at that moment.

I have family photographs of course, in lieu of a drawing, and here is one I found recently. It's a picture taken in the '50s by a professional photographer outside the fish and poultry shop that my dad managed in South Kensington, opposite Harrods. He is wearing his white shop coat, holding a pencil in his right hand and his order book, like a badge of office, in the other and you can just see a sales blackboard propped up in the doorway announcing: *Special – English Rabbits*. It looks as though he was working when the photographer asked him to step outside the shop onto the pavement of Brompton Road for the picture. I'm not sure why the photo was taken but it reminds me of those formal portraits of German society from the 1920s in August Sander's *People of the 20th Century*.

I have no idea who the slightly sinister-looking character is in the background, with his double-breasted suit and pocket handkerchief, he looks as though he has stepped straight out of a gangster film (who or what he was we'll never know). Perhaps it's his gaze and the cigarette smoke crossing the lower part of his face, or his black suit in contrast to my dad's white coat, that draws your eye to him, what is certain is that he has his own story which is lost to us. I'm sure if Sander had been taking the picture he would have told him to leave the frame.

I remember going with my dad several times when I was quite young, probably 10 or 12 years old, to Billingsgate. At four in the

morning the whole market was alive and as we went round everyone seemed to know him. An odd thing for me was that, although his name was Bill, all the traders called him Mr Chris or Chris, an affectionate shortening of his surname.

In Alex Danchev's *George Braque, A Life* I found this: 'Giacometti was prevailed upon to continue an ancient tradition and to make a drawing of Braque on his deathbed. In the still of the morning after (as it happened a Sunday), with Jean Leymarie in attendance for moral support, he struggled for several hours to discharge his responsibility to his satisfaction …Giacometti considered the result a failure. It was as if his subject refused to give up the ghost. "Each time I finished a drawing it was a living Braque. Curious, no?"'

At the end of your essay about the drawing of your father above your worktable you say, 'from being a site of departure, it has become a site of arrival. Every day more of my father's life returns to the drawing in front of me.'

I don't have a drawing as a magnet to attract memories but I do have a small gesture.

When I was growing up I used to watch my dad shaving, probably all boys do. To begin to shave means you are turning into a man. I watched him indirectly but carefully, to learn the tricks of the trade as it were, and one of the things he always did after putting the shaving soap on his face was to use the knuckle of the first finger on his left hand and draw it across his lips, from right to left, to clear the soap. I still do that each time I shave and every time I think of him.

With love from us all
John

from John Berger June 2011

15/6/11   Quincy
                                                          /.

Dear John,
        Yes, I knew Ossip Z. quite well,
and loved him a lot. And yes, I went I
see the Rotterdam monument in 1959. And I
wrote about it for him, I wanted him
to read words which behaved like his
branches and coats and handfuls of bronze.
I'm not sure whether we talked in French
n English.   Probably French and I understood
him easily because he spoke a slow, foreign,
Russian French.   He was like a mime -
with long-held precise movements and - at the
same time n in the same circus - he was
like a trapeze artist.   He had a physique,
body-proportions, which were somewhat similar to
Chaplin's - Chaplin in life before he
assumed his costumes.   Both mountebanks of
genius.   He was very good to me and
encouraged me and shook me when he saw
I was depressed.   Don't worry, he said,
so you decide to jump from the top of a
cliff by the sea, O.K. jump, and know
that an angel will hold your hand before
you are smashed to smithereens on the
rocks emerging from the waves!
        I like to think of that as I watch
his Accordeonist.   His instrument is like

an armful of books. There's something lightweight about Ossip — just as, by contrast, there's something heavyweight about Lipchitz. But let's remember that whatever weight you qualify for, it has nothing to do with skill, courage or profundity. Writing there ~~times~~ lines I feel the lightest touch of ~~his~~ Ossip's hand on my shoulder.

The Giacometti skull is also very light. We tend to forget how light skulls are, don't we? because for us most of the time their symbolism ~~weight~~ weighs them down.

My father when he died (suddenly) was eighty-four. As soon as I set eyes on him in his coffin, it was decided that I should draw him. I put it like that because it was'nt I who took the decision. It was a way of honouring him. of closing his life — as one closes the eyes of somebody who has died. I think the decision was taken at the moment (before I was born) when I wrote that poem, which is in our book, called Self-Portrait 1914-18.

In your so graphic account of your father's death you say you would'nt have had the courage to draw him. And I don't think that's right. Courage does'nt

Self-portrait
1914–18

———

It seems now that I was so near to that war.
I was born eight years after it ended
When the General Strike had been defeated.

Yet I was born by Very light and shrapnel
On duck boards
Among limbs without bodies.

I was born of the look of the dead
Swaddled in mustard gas
And fed in a dugout.

I was the groundless hope of survival
With mud between finger and thumb
Born near Abbeville.

I lived the first year of my life
Between the leaves of a pocket bible
Stuffed in a khaki haversack.

I lived the second year of my life
With three photos of a woman
Kept in a standard issue army paybook.

In the third year of my life
At 11 am on November 11th 1918
I became all that was conceivable.

Before I could see
Before I could cry out
Before I could go hungry

I was the world fit for heroes to live in.

4

70 .

(published in White Bird)

came into it. Your father was so young! His death was so sudden! And you absorbed the long brutal shock of it by getting on to your motorbike and driving, and then driving again with your mother as pillion, absorbing very, very, slightly _her_ shock!

In the photo of him standing outside the shop the likeness between you (both face and hands) is very clear. Perhaps he was less tall than you?

I used to watch sometimes my father shaving. Perhaps it was (still is?) a quite common ritual. An occasion for complicity and pride and conservation between father and son for being male. I can see my father sharpening his razor on a stone, like a tiny slate, in a sharpening box. I can see the Trenches sadness in his eyes as he looked into the mirror. I can see him brushing his elegant hair back for the day — to put a face on it. And I can see his total silence in which he knew that one day, despite all our conflicts and disagreements, I would be writing this. Like the total silence of the photo, your Dad in his boots in South Kensington.

Strange — no? — this silent exchange of a look which is totally without any coyness or self-consciousness. Compare your Dad's photo with Watteau's <u>Gilles</u>, the clown.

Two so different stories, in which, nevertheless, so much is the same. Look at the two right arms. Or the trouser bottoms or the eyes!

With love to you all

John.

Dear John

Yes, I knew Ossip Z. quite well and loved him a lot. And yes, I went to see the Rotterdam monument in 1959. And I wrote about it for him, I wanted him to read words which behaved like his branches and coats and handfuls of bronze. I'm not sure if we talked in French or English. Probably French and I understood him easily because he spoke a slow, foreign, Russian French. He was like a mime – with long-held precise movements and – at the same time or in the same circus – he was like a trapeze artist. He had a physique, body-proportions, which were somewhat similar to Chaplin's – Chaplin in life before he assumed his costumes. Both mountebanks of genius. He was very good to me and encouraged me and shook me when he saw I was depressed. Don't worry, he said, so you decide to jump from the top of a cliff by the sea, OK jump, and know that an angel will hold your hand before you are smashed to smithereens on the rocks emerging from the waves!

I like to think of that as I watch his *Accordionist*. His instrument is like an armful of books. There is something lightweight about Ossip – just as, by contrast, there is something heavyweight about Lipchitz. But let's remember that whatever weight you qualify for, it has nothing to do with skill, courage or profundity. Writing these lines I feel the lightest touch of Ossip's hand on my shoulder.

The Giacometti skull is also very light. We tend to forget how light skulls are, don't we? Because for us most of the time their symbolism weighs them down.

My father when he died (suddenly) was eighty-four. As soon as I set eyes on him in his coffin it was decided that I should draw him. I put it like that because it wasn't I who took the decision. It was a way of honouring him. Of closing his life – as one closes the eyes of somebody who has died. I think the decision was taken at the moment (before I was born) when I wrote that poem, which is in our book, called *Self-portrait 1914-18*.

In your so graphic account of your father's death you say you wouldn't have had the courage to draw him. And I don't think that is right. Courage doesn't come into it. Your father was so young! His death so sudden! And you absorbed the long brutal shock of it by getting on your motorbike and driving, and then driving again with your mother as pillion, absorbing very, very slightly her shock!

In the photo of him standing outside the shop the likeness between you (both face and hands) is very clear. Perhaps he was less tall than you?

I used to watch sometimes my father shaving. Perhaps it was (still is?) a quite common ritual. An occasion for complicity and pride and commiseration between father and son for being male. I can see my father sharpening his razor on a stone, like a tiny slate, in a sharpening box. I can see the Trenches' sadness in his eyes as he looked in the mirror. I can see him brushing his elegant hair back for the day – to put a face on it. And I can see his total silence in which he knew that one day, despite our conflicts and disagreements, I would be writing this. Like the total silence of the photo of your Dad in his boots in South Kensington.

Strange – no? – this silent exchange of a look which is totally without any coyness or self-consciousness. Compare your Dad's photo with Watteau's *Gilles*, the clown.

Two so different stories in which, nevertheless, so much is the same. Look at the two right arms. Or the trouser bottoms or the eyes!

With love to you all
John

Self-portrait 1914-18

It seems now that I was so near to that war.
I was born eight years after it ended
When the General Strike had been defeated.

Yet I was born by Very Light and shrapnel
On duck boards
Among limbs without bodies.

I was born of the look of the dead
Swaddled in mustard gas
And fed in a dugout.

I was the groundless hope of survival
With mud between finger and thumb
Born near Abbeville.

I lived the first year of my life
Between the leaves of a pocket bible
Stuffed in a khaki haversack.

I lived the second year of my life
With three photos of a woman
Kept in a standard issue army paybook.

In the third year of my life
At 11am on November 11th 1918
I became all that was conceivable.

Before I could see
Before I could cry out
Before I could go hungry

I was the world fit for heroes to live in.

from John Christie November 2011

A Circular Walk

I constantly came up against a borderline where I felt, well, if I could go a little bit further it might get very interesting, that is, if I were allowed to make things up. That temptation to work with only very fragmentary pieces of evidence, to fill in the gaps and blank spaces and create out of this a meaning that is greater than that you can't prove, led me to work in a way which wasn't determined by any discipline.

W. G. Sebald in conversation with Christophe Bigsby

Dear John

Yesterday evening, with your letter in my pocket, I set off on a walk around the wood that faces us across the fields. After a poor summer the weather now in late September is sunny and warm. It's a shame to be indoors and as I'd been in the studio most of the day I needed to stretch my legs and this is a walk I often do.

The public footpath which passes the back of our garden takes me, if I turn right and head east, on a circular route with, for most of the time, the neighbouring farmer's wood on my right. The wood itself, about 60 acres, is out of bounds. There are plenty of paths into it but all have a sign at their beginning that says PRIVATE – walkers are not encouraged to cross that PRIVATE/PUBLIC threshold. Occasionally I can catch sight of a herd of deer in the shade amongst the trees. We watch each other quietly through the foliage until one of the animals breaks the gaze between us and they move silently off and disappear.

One of the joys of this walk is seeing the hares which, against the freshly ploughed fields, are clearly visible. I try to walk as silently as I can on the grass of the path, avoiding the patches of gravel, and this way can sometimes almost trip over one of them before it races off across the open ground. In the middle of the field, a safe distance from me, it will stop, ears up, to see if I'm following before relaxing slightly and lolloping off into the nearest cover. On a spring evening I've seen them boxing on the edge of the wood, something I thought was just part of the mythology that surrounds the hare. I wonder why these creatures have this powerful mythical quality which seems to exist in every culture

Crouching hare, Roman Empire C. AD 1-200

from East to West; the hare as trickster, shape-shifter and familiar of the supernatural?

There is a small Roman bronze hare in the Sainsbury collection, tense and ready to run – if a little fatter than the ones in the fields near the house.

It says in the catalogue that this figure was probably an ornamental attachment to a larger object like a table rather than an individual piece for display. It's small, just over 4 inches long, and would fit comfortably in my pocket alongside your letter. Although the inlay is missing now, originally this hare's eyes must have shone when they caught the light.

Watteau - 'gilles' c1718-19

I carried with me too on the walk, in your letter, Watteau's *Gilles* and the memory of my dad. Since you pointed out the similarities of pose between the photo and Watteau's painting I spent some time reading about and looking at reproductions of *Gilles*. Watteau painted it around 1718 and, so the reference book says, it is thought to have been perhaps a sign for the café run by a former actor, Belloni, who had made his name as a Pierrot.

Whatever the original purpose of the painting it is a haunting image. In his ill-fitting costume, with its over-long, rucked-up sleeves and short trousers Gilles stands before us a rather awkward figure, looking to me like someone who has been pushed on-stage, unprepared and against their will. Or perhaps it is an audition and he's suffering from stage-fright?

He doesn't inhabit the clothes or strike a pose like an experienced actor, for example like the player in red to the right of the picture, but just stands there in his costume in a rather self-conscious way. He also seems to be isolated from the others, who take no notice of him. It's as though, looking at the reproduction, they are characters on the painted backcloth behind him. Across his young face flickers the hint of a question.

Marcel Nicoud

My dad in comparison seems totally at home in his
work clothes, the shortness of the trousers ensuring
that the bottoms were well away from the puddles
of water on the fish shop floor and, as he is the
manager, he wears a tie. It reminds me a little of
that photo of Marcel that Jean took, Marcel's
'official portrait', where he brushed his hair and
dressed smartly from the waist up but still had
his cowshit-covered work trousers and boots on
just out of the frame: 'And now my great grandchildren will know what kind of a man I was'.

Although of course I realise that Gilles is
dressed for theatrical effect and my dad for work
both pictures contain their own mystery, either
could be the starting point of a story – the
character behind my dad wearing, conveniently for
say a mystery story, a black suit to contrast with
my dad's white coat – a dark nemesis at his back.

With the contents of a street photo we have the
beauty of this kind of chance happening but we know
that chance doesn't come into the Watteau, everything is there because the painter painstakingly
put it there. The theatrical, badly-fitting
clothes, the look on Gilles' young face, his gauche
stance, all put there for a purpose, questions
posed by Watteau telling a story that we can only
speculate about.

I've just been rereading *Railtracks* and was struck
by the connections of memory that link so quickly
as one thought sets off another and then another.
The book immediately brought back memories of your
performance with Anne Michaels in the German
Gymnasium at King's Cross in 2005. I remember the
whole audience at one point being directed to
cross the dark room to look out onto the old,
restored railway worker's tenements; the actress
descending from the ceiling, uncoiling slowly from
above on that gym rope as you and Anne sat facing
each other across the table.

Part of your text describes drawing at Willesden
Junction with Pru Clough. I met her only once,
briefly, quite a few years ago, at a friend's
house and would have loved to ask her about those
Willesden expeditions and about her aunt, Eileen
Gray, too. There is another connection in your
description of the discarded workman's gloves she
found in the rail yard:

'She tried them on, laughing. They were huge and her wrists, like her legs, were very thin. She was the best painter of her generation.' I wanted to read then that she'd taken the gloves back to her studio instead of leaving them in a conspicuous place to be found again. The reason for that is another connection. At Derrick and Sally Greaves' house, just outside Norwich, is a collage by Pru which has a pair of old work gloves attached to it. I was hoping these might have been the same gloves, resurfacing. All these small points of memory connecting.

W. g. Sebald said in an interview:
" Memory resides in details of
this almost weightless kind."

I was hunting through my books in the studio the other day and I came across a large Thames and Hudson monograph on Modigliani, a birthday present when I was 15. Why was I attracted to his work as a teenager? Probably because the images were accessible to me, sexy in some cases, and also perhaps because of the legend of his bohemian life.

I'd seen his three works in the gallery on previous visits, a painting and two drawings, and I read a new biography about him to refresh my memory although it wasn't much help in the end to understanding his work. It rather played up a dissolute lifestyle which didn't seem to be much of a problem for those that actually knew him.

Modigliani 1918

Gino Severini comments on this in his autobiography:
'...it would be an error to believe that
Modigliani's brilliance, vivacity, and interest in
his surroundings at any given moment of his life
were produced by stimulants. Everyone in
Montparnasse was fond of him and not because of his
rare moments of excess after having had a couple of
absinthes in the course of an evening. Instead he
was liked for his natural self, for the personality
visible in his day-to-day relationships with
companions at any point of the day.'

I thought I'd go to Norwich and look at the three works again. It was a Friday and the gallery was more crowded and noisier than usual with quite a few visiting school children.

Two are portraits of the same person, Anna Zborowski, the wife of Modigliani's dealer, done within a year or so of each other, 1917-19. They are very recognisably the same woman. The drawing of her has the feeling, and I don't know if Modigliani actually worked like this, of being drawn initially without taking his eye off the model, the pencil moving in the arc of his wrist or forearm. In the painting Anna Z's face, which has precise pencil marks drawn over the pigment (the line of the nose and the outline of the lips) seems divided into two vertical parts, the left with its blank eye faces you directly while the other, the 'seeing' side, looks off a little to the viewer's right, the nose slightly in profile. Perhaps this ambiguity of focus is what gives the portrait its air of waiting, as though she has just asked a question and now it is your turn, she is waiting for an answer. Perhaps these are works, unlike the Watteau, that don't provoke a story?

But it is the eyes that I find fascinating because he manages to suggest substance and character with blankness. This especially applies to the drawings where the blankness of the eye is the untouched paper, so it can also read as a hole in the drawing.

Unlike Giacometti's self-portrait, where the pupil had been drawn in and then erased, this eye has been left blank, or coloured pupil-less in the case of the painting. In the drawing where the white of the eye is the white of the paper, it becomes like the eye-hole in a mask.

Head of a Woman (Anna Zborowska) 1918 or 19

In fact, surrounding Modigliani's work in the collection are masks from every culture and the power of them changes depending whether you can see light on the background beyond the mask (so it appears empty) or if shadow gives the impression that the mask is inhabited. Not too far from the painting of Anna Zborowski in the display is a green jade Olmec mask from Mexico which caught my attention. Because of the lighting, and the height and angle you choose to view it from, it shows this empty/inhabited effect as you approach it.

Olmec Jade mask - Mexico 900-600 BC

portrait of a woman (Anna Zborowska) c. 1917

There is one other Modigliani drawing on display, a large *Caryatid* from a few years earlier, 1913, when he was still struggling with sculpture. Around the delicate pencil drawing of the figure, the outline has been emphasised, uncharacteristically, with thick, rough crayon lines like gouge marks giving the effect of a carved relief. I really like this drawing because he manages to undermine the power and strength of the sculptural image by turning her back from stone into a real woman with the tiny mark indicating her navel and the outward twist of her left ankle.

It's interesting to see how unsuccessful he was in his lifetime but how rapidly his fame and the prices of his work rose after his death.

In my catalogue of the Tate show of his work in 1963 John Russell notes in his introduction what he detects as a tradition of English sympathy for Modigliani and his work. It seems that Augustus John was the first person to buy one of his sculptures and that Modigliani took part in an exhibition in London, 'French Art 1914-19', six months before he died. This show, organised by the Sitwell brothers at the Mansard Gallery on the top floor of Heal's in Tottenham Court Road included the work of Picasso, Derain, Matisse and your friend Ossip Zadkine. Modigliani had the largest number of works on display and sold paintings to, amongst others, Arnold Bennett. His drawings were for sale for one shilling each!

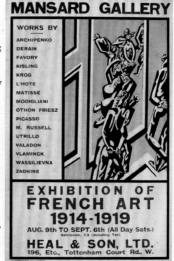

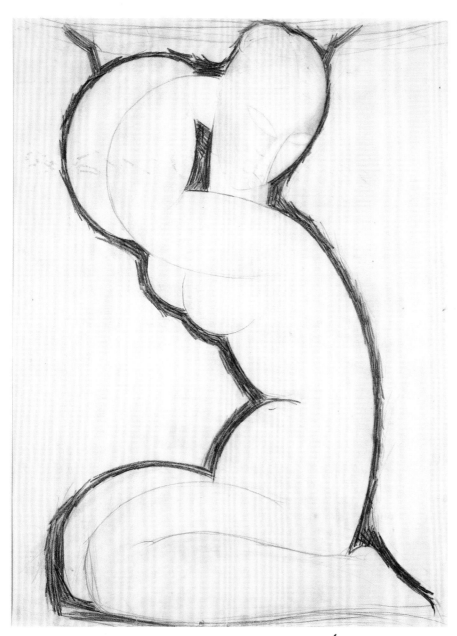

Caryatid c 1913

Anna Z. with Bacon's 'Portrait of P.L' 1957

Although Modigliani is not an artist
I've thought about much since the 1960s.
by spending time and looking closely
at these three works in the collection
I've grown to love them, they are beautiful.
Although his faces, it seems to me, have
some of the properties of masks perhaps
coming from his earlier interest in
African sculpture, they are not
concealing or hiding the person but
the opposite, they reveal and have
a humanity and serenity about
them which makes them so
self-contained.
Hanging a few feet behind the portrait
of Anna Z is a large study for a

portrait of Peter Lacey by Francis Bacon.
Here it looks as though a human mask
has been stripped away to reveal an
almost beast-like persona behind -
there is not a great deal of serenity here!
I went back and read your Modigliani
essay in "White Bird" and you say at
one point: 'in themselves his paintings
demand little explanation. Indeed they
impose a kind of silence, a listening'.
Perhaps this is why I've had trouble
trying to see into those portraits, why
the idea of the mask formed in my
thoughts. Sightless eyes in sculpture
do not bother me and in a funny way
this drawing and painting of Anna Z
feel like sculptures I've been able to
walk around.
But having circled Modigliani the
experience takes me back to the
farmer's wood: beautiful, peaceful
and intriguing from the outside I've
peered through the foliage to try to
glimpse what's going on but haven't
been allowed in.

with love from us all   John.

Dear John

Yesterday evening, with your letter in my pocket, I set off on a walk around the wood that faces us across the fields. After a poor summer the weather now in late September is sunny and warm. It's a shame to be indoors and as I'd been in the studio most of the day I needed to stretch my legs and this is a walk I often do.

The public footpath which passes the back of our garden takes me, if I turn right and head east, on a circular route with, for most of the time, the neighbouring farmer's wood on my right. The wood itself, about 60 acres, is out of bounds. There are plenty of paths into it but all have a sign at their beginning that says PRIVATE – walkers are not encouraged to cross that PRIVATE/PUBLIC threshold. Occasionally I can catch sight of a herd of deer in the shade amongst the trees. We watch each other quietly through the foliage until one of the animals breaks the gaze between us and they move silently off and disappear.

One of the joys of this walk is seeing the hares which, against the freshly ploughed fields, are clearly visible. I try to walk as silently as I can on the grass of the path, avoiding the patches of gravel, and this way can sometimes almost trip over one of them before it races off across the open ground. In the middle of the field, a safe distance from me, it will stop, ears up, to see if I'm following before relaxing slightly and lolloping off into the nearest cover. On a spring evening I've seen them boxing on the edge of the wood, something I thought was just part of the mythology that surrounds the hare. I wonder why these creatures have this powerful mythical quality which seems to exist in every culture from East to West; the hare as trickster, shape-shifter and familiar of the supernatural?

There is a small Roman bronze hare in the Sainsbury collection, tense and ready to run – if a little fatter than the ones in the fields near the house. It says in the catalogue that this figure was probably an ornamental attachment to a larger object like a table rather than an individual piece for display. It's small, just over four inches long, and would fit comfortably in my pocket alongside your letter. Although the inlay is missing now, originally this hare's eyes must have shone when they caught the light.

I carried with me too on the walk, in your letter, Watteau's *Gilles* and the memory of my dad. Since you pointed out the similarities of pose between the photo and Watteau's painting I spent some time reading about and looking at reproductions of *Gilles*. Watteau painted it around 1718 and, so the reference book says, it is thought to have been perhaps a sign for the café run by a former actor, Belloni, who had made his name as a Pierrot.

Whatever the original purpose of the painting it is a haunting image. In his ill-fitting costume, with its over-long, rucked-up sleeves and short trousers Gilles stands before us a rather awkward figure, looking to me like someone who has been pushed on-stage, unprepared and against their will. Or perhaps it is an audition and he's suffering from stage-fright? He doesn't inhabit the clothes or strike a pose like an experienced actor, for example like the player in red to the right of the picture, but just stands there in his costume in a rather self-conscious way. He also seems to be isolated from the others, who take no notice of him. It's as though, looking at the reproduction, they are characters on the painted backcloth behind him. Across his young face flickers the hint of a question.

My dad in comparison seems totally at home in his work clothes, the shortness of the trousers ensuring that the bottoms were well away from the puddles of water on the fish shop floor and, as he is the manager, he wears a tie.

It reminds me a little of that photo of Marcel that Jean (Mohr) took, Marcel's 'official portrait', where he brushed his hair and dressed smartly from the waist up but still had his cowshit-covered work trousers and boots on just out of the frame: 'And now my great grandchildren will know what kind of a man I was'.

Although of course I realise that Gilles is dressed for theatrical effect and my dad for work both pictures contain their own mystery, either could be the starting point of a story – the character behind my dad wearing, conveniently for, say, a mystery story, a black suit to contrast with my dad's white coat – a dark nemesis at his back.

With the contents of a street photo we have the beauty of this kind of chance happening but we know that chance doesn't come into the Watteau, everything is there because the painter painstakingly put it there. The theatrical, badly-fitting clothes, the look on Gilles' young face, his gauche stance, all put there for a purpose, questions posed by Watteau telling a story that we can only speculate about.

I've just been reading *Railtracks* and was struck by the connections of memory that link so quickly as one thought sets off another and then another. The book immediately brought back memories of your performance with Anne Michaels in the German Gymnasium at King's Cross in 2005. I remember the whole audience at one point being directed to cross the dark room to look out onto the old, restored railway worker's tenements; the actress descending from the ceiling, uncoiling slowly from above on that gym rope as you and Anne sat facing each other across the table.

Part of your text describes drawing at Willesden Junction with Pru Clough. I met her only once, briefly, quite a few years ago, at a friend's house and would have loved to ask her about those Willesden expeditions and about her aunt, Eileen Gray, too. There is another connection in your description of the discarded workman's gloves she found in the rail yard:
'She tried them on, laughing. They were huge and her wrists, like her legs, were very thin. She was the best painter of her generation.'
I wanted to read then that she'd taken the gloves back to her studio instead of leaving them in a conspicuous place to be found again.

At Derrick and Sally Greaves' house, just outside Norwich, is a collage by Pru which has a pair of old work gloves attached to it. I was hoping these might have been the same gloves, resurfacing. All these small points of memory connecting.

W. G. Sebald said in an interview: 'Memory resides in details of this almost weightless kind.'

I was hunting through my books in the studio the other day and I came across a large Thames and Hudson monograph on Modigliani, a birthday present when I was 15. Why was I attracted to his work as a teenager? Probably because the images were accessible to me, sexy in some cases, and also perhaps because of the legend of his bohemian life.

I'd seen his three works in the gallery on previous visits, a painting and two drawings, and I read a new biography about him to refresh my memory although it wasn't much help in the end to understanding his work. It rather played up a dissolute lifestyle which didn't seem to be much of a problem for those that actually knew him.

Gino Severini comments on this in his autobiography:

'... it would be an error to believe that Modigliani's brilliance, vivacity, and interest in his surroundings at any given moment of his life were produced by stimulants. Everyone in Montparnasse was fond of him and not because of his rare moments of excess after having had a couple of absinthes in the course of an evening. Instead he was liked for his natural self, for the personality visible in his day-to-day relationships with companions at any point of the day.'

I thought I'd go to Norwich and look at the three works again. It was a Friday and the gallery was more crowded and noisier than usual with quite a few visiting school children.

Two are portraits of the same person, Anna Zborowski, the wife of Modigliani's dealer, done within a year or so of each other, 1917-19. They are very recognisably the same woman. The drawing of her has the feeling, and I don't know if Modigliani actually worked like this, of being drawn initially without taking his eye off the model, the pencil moving in the arc of his wrist or forearm. In the painting Anna Z's face, which has precise pencil marks drawn over the pigment (the line of the nose and the outline of the lips) seems divided into two vertical parts, the left with its blank eye faces you directly while the other, the 'seeing' side, looks off a little to the viewer's right, the nose slightly in profile. Perhaps this ambiguity of focus is what gives the portrait its air of waiting, as though she has just asked a question and now it is your turn, she is waiting for an answer. Perhaps these are works, unlike the Watteau, that don't provoke a story?

But it is the eyes that I find fascinating because he manages to suggest substance and character with blankness. This especially applies to the drawings where the blankness of the eye is the untouched paper, so it can also read as a hole in the drawing.

Unlike Giacometti's self-portrait, where the pupil had been drawn in and then erased, this eye has been left blank, or coloured pupil-less in the case of the painting. In the drawing where the white of the eye is the white of the paper, it becomes like the eye-hole in a mask.

In fact, surrounding Modigliani's work in the collection are masks from every culture and the power of them changes depending whether you can see light on the background beyond the mask (so it appears empty) or if shadow gives the impression that the mask is inhabited. Not too far from the painting of Anna Zborowski in the display is a green jade Olmec mask from Mexico which caught my attention. Because of the lighting, and the height and angle you choose to view it from, it shows this empty/inhabited effect as you approach it.

There is one other Modigliani drawing on display, a large *Caryatid* from a few years earlier, 1913, when he was still struggling with sculpture. Around the delicate pencil drawing of the figure, the outline has been emphasised, uncharacteristically, with thick, rough crayon lines like gouge marks giving the effect of a carved relief. I really like this drawing because he manages to undermine the power and strength of the sculptural image by turning her back from stone into a real woman with the tiny mark indicating her navel and the outward twist of her left ankle.

It's interesting to see how unsuccessful he was in his lifetime but how rapidly his fame and the prices of his work rose after his death.

In my catalogue of the Tate show of his work in 1963 John Russell notes in his introduction what he detects as a tradition of English sympathy for Modigliani and his work. It seems that Augustus John was the first person to buy one of his sculptures and that Modigliani took part in an exhibition in London, 'French Art 1914-19', six months before he died. This show, organised by the Sitwell brothers at the Mansard Gallery on the top floor of Heal's in Tottenham Court Road included the work of Picasso, Derain, Matisse and your friend Ossip Zadkine. Modigliani had the largest number of works on display and sold paintings to, amongst others, Arnold Bennett. His drawings were for sale for one shilling each!

Although Modigliani is not an artist I've thought about much since the 1960s, by spending time and looking closely at these three works I've grown to love them, they are beautiful. Although his faces, it seems to me, have some of the properties of masks, perhaps coming from his earlier interest and study of African sculpture, they are not concealing or hiding the person but the opposite, they reveal and have a humanity and serenity about them which makes them so self-contained.

Hanging a few feet behind the portrait of Anna Z is a large study for a portrait of Peter Lacey by Francis Bacon. Here it looks as though a human mask has been stripped away to reveal an almost beast-like persona behind – there's not a great deal of serenity here.

I went back and read your Modigliani essay in *White Bird* and you say at one point: 'In themselves his paintings demand little explanation. Indeed they impose a kind of silence, a listening'. Perhaps this is why I've had trouble trying to see into those

portraits, why the idea of the mask formed in my thoughts. Sightless eyes in sculpture do not bother me and in a funny way this drawing and painting of Anna Z feel like sculptures I've been able to walk around. But having circled Modigliani the experience takes me back to the farmer's private wood; beautiful, peaceful and intriguing from the outside I've peered through the foliage to try to glimpse what's going on but haven't been allowed in.

With love from us all
John

from John Berger December 2011

/12/11   Quincy

John,
    There's a short poem by WB Yeats,
written around 1919, which has remained in
my mind (N heart) ever since I first read
it when I was in my teens. And I
remember it because of the hare — the
hare who has disappeared and yet is so
present.

> One had a lovely face,
> And two or three had charm,
> But charm and face were in vain
> Because the mountain grass
> Cannot but keep the form
> Where the mountain hare has lain.

    Why, you ask, is the hare a legendary
animal in so many stories and cultures?
Does'nt it have something to do with the
hare's nonchalence? The visible nonchalence that
allows her N him to be free. The word
nonchalence comes from the old French word
nonchaloir : to disregard. And chaloir
comes from the Latin Calere : to be warm. Today
the term for nonchalent is cool. Hares have
always been cool, no? The Roman bronze

2

If a crouching one shows him (he's male for sure) keeping his cool.

I love the idea that Watteau's Gilles was painted as a sign for a café. "See you at Gilles on Friday night". As for the performer's "awkwardness", I think it's a question of the moment that Watteau wanted to depict. The Gilles is just about to step forward into the limelight, into view. What will be funny and disarming is at this instant, when he is gathering himself together and amassing his energy, just awkward and apparently helpless. Don't all great comics step forward out of a total helplessness, and isn't this why we identify with them?

Your Dad, by contrast, has just stepped outside after a highly successful performance. Nearly all the fish sold, and time to change and go home. Like every morning he was up early this morning.

Pru got up early too I think. She was a very systematic worker. She was highly independant but not bohemian; for her, bohemianism was a form of exhibitionism. Suddenly as I write this I want to see a photo of her and I cant find one. You

want me to tell more about Pru and I can't.
We had a secret together, a deep secret and
I can't tell it. Partly because to do so ~~would~~
might be a kind of betrayal, and partly because
I can't put this secret into words even to
keep to myself. What passed between us, what
we did together, what we gave to one another
we never described or named or qualified. And
for the two of us this was a measure of its
depth — or height. P.// As if the two of us
were putting up or dismantling scaffolding. Every
action is noted and replied to but words don't
carry — and, anyway, they get blown away in
the wind. Sometimes she painted the scaffolding
Sometimes ~~a~~ I coloured a single short pole
bright red and her eyes would twinkle. A
clough in old English means a ravine or deep
valley. She had ~~very~~ the little nostrils ~~~~ of a stoat,
And our little fingers were interchangeable.

" Memory resides in details of this
almost weightless kind."

I love your collage of different views
of the Mexican jade mask ; it says so much
about the expression of a presence and the secret
of that presence.

4.

You have made me think — not for the first
time — hard about Modigliani. As in your
story, he first impressed me when I was
adolescent. Fourteen maybe. He was sexy
and he was also frontal, frank. He was the
opposite of evasive. Later when I was at
art-school he influenced the way I tried to
paint, particularly portraits and nudes. The
search for a profile rather than an atmospheric
suggestion. To render a face as if it were
a word written with its own unique alphabet.
So that a painting of somebody becomes like her
or his own signature! And he was born
in Livorno, which I visited in 1947 and which
became for me a legendary city, a city of.

survival. Here's a painting I made, following that visit.

John Berger, Street Acrobat, 1949, Livorno, Italy

VIII ⑥.

/ Your question remains: what to make of
the emptiness of expression in Modigliani's
painted figures — it is not as though he
was a withdrawn or cold man, far from it.
Their eyes are like those of statues, and he
thought of himself first and foremost as a
sculptor. Yet it is not only their eyes
which are empty of expression — it's also
their mouths and other features. ~~Yet it~~
At the same time these figures are more
intimately present than most painted figures.
They are there, as I say, like their own
handwritten signatures. What lies behind
this paradox?

I have two ideas. When Modigliani
wanted to paint somebody he wanted to strip
them. Whether man or woman. Whether portrait
or nude. He wanted them stripped down to
their bare skin. Without disguise. And
in his fervour in doing this he
stripped away anything that was circumstantial:
garments, expressions, glances, active
gestures. He wanted his painted figures
to be immaculate, spotless. In a
very strange way (considering their lives)
Fra Angelico was perhaps Modigliani's soul mate.

My second idea involves his own health. From childhood onwards he was dogged by illness, and when he died he was thirty six years old. He was not a hypochondriac but he was more aware than most of the proximity and constant threat of death. And he responded to this by imagining, creating, ~~studen~~ studying, deathless stone figures who could outlive temples and hold them up — caryatids, or, else, the carved wooden figures of goddesses from the Ivory Coast, or else Gothic statues from the cathedrals. Such figures were, by both function and definition, above the trivia of daily life and the hassle of changeing moods. They watch us with a certain benevolence, but of themselves they show us almost nothing. And for him they were a model.

~~And~~ So you are reminded of the forest you are forbidden to enter — And of the hares who are nonchalant, inconsequent and go where they please. Pru was'nt hare-lipped, but her tiny nostrils could quiver like a hare's.

With love to you all in the barn.

John

John

There's a short poem by W. B. Yeats, written around 1919, which has remained in my mind (or heart) ever since I first read it when I was in my teens. And I remember it because of the hare – the hare who has disappeared and yet is so present.

> One had a lovely face,
> And two or three had charm,
> But charm and face were in vain
> Because the mountain grass
> Cannot but keep the form
> Where the mountain hare has lain.

Why, you ask, is the hare a legendary animal in so many stories and cultures? Doesn't it have something to do with the hare's nonchalance? The visible nonchalance that allows her or him to be free. The word *nonchalance* comes from the old French word *nonchaloir*: to disregard. And *chaloir* comes from the Latin *celare*: to be warm. Today the term for nonchalant is cool. Hares have always been cool, no? The Roman bronze of a crouching one shows him (he's male for sure) keeping his cool.

I love the idea that Watteau's *Gilles* was painted as a sign for a café. 'See you at Gilles on Friday night'. As for the performer's 'awkwardness', I think it's a question of the moment that Watteau wanted to depict. Gilles is just about to step forward into the limelight, into view. What will be funny and disarming at this instant, when he is gathering himself together and amassing his energy, just awkward and apparently helpless. Don't all great comics step forward out of a total helplessness, and isn't this why we identify with them?

Your dad, by contrast, has just stepped outside after a highly successful performance. Nearly all the fish sold, and time to change and go home. Like every morning he was up early this morning.

Pru got up early too I think. She was a highly systematic worker. She was highly independent but not bohemian; for her bohemianism was a form of exhibitionism. Suddenly as I write this I want to see a photo of her and I can't find one. You want me to tell you more about Pru and I can't. We had a secret together, a deep secret and I can't tell it. Partly because to do so might be a kind of betrayal, and partly because I can't put this secret into words even to keep to myself. What passed between us, what we did together, what we gave to one another we never described or named or qualified. And for the two of us this was a measure of its depth – or height.

As if the two of us were putting up or dismantling scaffolding. Every action is noted and replied to but words don't carry – and, anyway, they get blown away in the wind. Sometimes she painted the scaffolding in her pictures. Sometimes I coloured a single short pole bright red and her eyes would twinkle. A clough in Old English means a ravine or deep valley. She had the little nostrils of a stoat. And our little fingers were interchangeable.

'Memory resides in details of this almost weightless kind.'

I love your collage of different views of the Mexican jade mask; it says so much about the expression of a presence and the secret of that presence.

You have made me think – not for the first time – hard about Modigliani. As in your story he first impressed me when I was an adolescent. Fourteen maybe. He was sexy and he was also frontal, frank. He was the opposite of evasive. Later when I was at art school he influenced the way I tried to paint, particularly portraits and nudes. The search for a profile rather than an atmospheric suggestion. To render a face as if it were a word written with its own unique alphabet. So that a painting of somebody becomes like her or his signature! And he was born in Livorno, which I visited in 1947 and which for me became a legendary city, a city of survival. Here is a painting that I made following that visit.

Your question remains: what to make of the emptiness of expression in Modigliani's painted figures – it is not as though he was a withdrawn or cold man. Their eyes are like those of statues, and he thought of himself first and foremost as a sculptor. Yet it is not only their eyes which are empty of expression – it's also their mouths and other features. At the same time these figures are more intimately present than most painted figures, they are there, as I say, like their own handwritten signatures. What lies behind this paradox?

I have two ideas. When Modigliani wanted to paint somebody he wanted to strip them. Whether man or woman. Whether the portrait or nude. He wanted them stripped down to their bare skin. Without disguise. And in his fervour in doing this he stripped away everything that was circumstantial: garments, expressions, glances, active gestures. He wanted his painted figures to be immaculate, spotless. In a very strange way (considering their lives) Fra Angelico was perhaps Modigliani's soul mate.

My second idea involves his own health. From childhood onwards he was dogged by illness, and when he died he was thirty-six years old. He was not a hypochondriac but he was more aware than most of the proximity and constant threat of death. And he responded to this by imagining, creating, studying, deathless stone figures who could outlive temples and hold them up – caryatids, or else the carved wooden figures of goddesses from the Ivory Coast, or else Gothic statues from the cathedrals. Such figures were, by both function and definition, above the trivia of daily life and the hassle of changing moods. They watch us with a certain benevolence, but of themselves they show us almost nothing. And for him they were a model.

So you are reminded of the forest you are forbidden to enter – and of the hares who are nonchalant, inconsequent and go where they please. Pru wasn't hare-lipped, but her tiny nostrils could quiver like a hare's.

With love to you all in the barn

from John Christie February 2012

Hiding in Plain View

Mean something! You and I, mean something!
Ah, that's a good one!

Samuel Beckett quoted by R.B.Kitaj in notes on
his painting *Dismantling the Red Tent*

Last weekend it snowed quite hard overnight and the low daily temperatures mean that the covering of snow has lingered on. Walking my usual route around the wood today surrounded by white fields I could see evidence of animals everywhere, thousands of small footprints (there's a Suffolk dialect word for them, *feetings*) but no creatures in sight, frightened away probably, if they had been nearby, by the sound of my boots compacting the frozen snow. It was impossible to walk silently and my footsteps carried across the open ground and into the darkness of the wood. As the footpath crossed the fields I did have the luck to see a barn owl. I spotted him some way off and waited, quite still on the open path willing him to come towards me, while he patrolled the ditch around the edge of the field. Gradually he came nearer to the spot where I stood. He was only feet away, almost, it felt, close enough to touch, when his eyes flicked up from searching the ground and noticed me. A sharp change of direction and he was silently away across the snow to carry on hunting in private.

For some reason Livorno was in my mind, perhaps because I'd been thinking about your letter and your connection with the city, Modigliani's birthplace, and I had the vague recollection that your book *G* begins there. When I got home I checked and there it was, Livorno, in the second line. Holding the book again reminded me of what a good job Richard Hollis had made of the design – the jacket still looks striking and distinctive. Later editions unfortunately didn't fair so well. There's another small connection with Livorno and *Bento's Sketchbook* that I remember. Modigliani's mother claimed Spinoza as one of her family's Jewish ancestors, through a blood line from the philosopher's younger brother. I'm not sure where I read that but I hope, for connectivity, it's true.

I mentioned that Sunday lunch in the early 90s with Pru Clough and you said you couldn't find a photo of her. Well here is a picture from that day that my friends have unearthed, it was in February, near Valentine's Day, we think. Perhaps that way of holding her hand and the cigarette is familiar to you? Did you ever do any drawings of each other?

I called in to see Derrick and Sally the other day
on my way back from Norwich. He had some new work
on the go that I was keen to see and also I wanted
to take a photo of Pru's work-glove collage.

I discovered that my memory had played a trick on
me and there wasn't a pair, just one glove with a
large nail fixing it to the back board - perhaps
she'd gone back later to retrieve it from the
Goods Yard?

Up until the mid-90s most of my graphic work, if that is the right word, took the form of books and prints made, mainly at Circle Press, between times when I wasn't filming. It was a good arrangement as long as the gap between camerawork and directing jobs didn't get too long and the money too thin.

I was thinking about this work balance the other day as I watched the light changing in my studio. At this time of the year the sun is at such a low angle that it comes skating straight in and, because of the strong shadows, makes it difficult to work unless the sunlight is softened with tracing paper over the windows.

I watched the shadows slowly crossing my drawing board as the sun began to go down. When I turned the overhead lights on the atmosphere in the space changed again and I realised that for most of my working life I've been thinking about light, collecting the memories of how light falls in a room or on a face. Sometimes it was a very conscious activity as when considering and planning how to light a particular scene for a drama. But mostly it was something I'd trained myself to do automatically – remembering a pleasing or unusual combination of light; how tungsten light mixed with daylight in a room; how soft light wrapped itself around an object; how a room could be animated by shadows from action outside the frame. I stored these effects in my memory for later, for the time they might come in useful. The film lighting I enjoyed doing most was the kind that didn't draw attention to itself, where the scene or the portrait appeared not to be lit at all except by natural light.

Now, instead of light, I work mostly with paper
and coloured pastels, a medium I took up after I
came back from a trip to Australia in 2000. I'd
been invited to make a print at the art school in
Canberra and wanting to try to come to the subject
afresh I didn't take any visual material with me
from home. I did take in my notebook a quotation
from the Australian architect Glenn Murcutt, a
simple instruction, originating I think from an
observation by Thoreau, so that buildings might
sit harmoniously in the landscape:
*Take a handful of earth at your feet and paint
your house that colour*

That phrase took me to the beginnings of an idea
for the print. Flying for hours on end over the
countryside and seeing the colouring of red iron
oxide and yellow ochre in the expanses of the
landscape I decided to use these earth colours,
which I found so beautiful, for my Australian
print.

On my first day in Canberra (I'd been in Perth
for the previous week) everywhere in the city was
fairly empty because people were sitting at home
watching the Sydney Olympics on TV. That morning,
to push the travelling out of my head, I went to
look around the National Gallery. On the way back
to my flat in the art school I picked up, on the
banks of the lake outside the gallery, another
element I thought might help me to begin next
day, a bunch of dried gum tree leaves. I had some
great practical help from the team in the print
workshop and we finished the edition in a few
days before I headed back to London.

In the middle of this letter I've made a version
of that print for you, with pastel providing the
colours instead of the original earth pigments.

I brought some bags of coloured earth home with me but in the studio found the powder very difficult to control – it went everywhere and it was then that I turned to pastel. I could match any of the earth colours with a pastel and they were much easier to handle than the raw powder.

As I got more technically used to working with pastel I increased my colour range from those initial earth pigments and also began to make small wooden constructions. Sometimes the construction came first, sometimes the pastel on paper. The form of the work looked to European Constructivism but I tried to see if I could introduce the idea of changing viewpoints and depth to the works on paper, something I could do with a 3D construction just by moving the position of my head. These changes in my work came in part from the discovery of 'Dazzle' camouflage at the Imperial War Museum in London. This was the Navy's practical solution, introduced towards the end of World War One and used well into the Second, of disguising ships at sea with disruptive patterning to confuse the eye – a way to hide them in plain view.

British Dazzle ships with bunting celebrating the armistice 1918

During the period from March to December 1917
German submarines sank on average more than 23
Allied ships each week, a total of over 900 ships.
At the beginning of the war when a U-boat attacked
an enemy ship the submarine would surface, making
it vulnerable to attack, and fire on the ship
with its deck-mounted cannon. If the target was
an unarmed merchant ship, the submarine would
pull alongside, evacuate everyone on board into
the lifeboats before sinking the ship. Merchant
vessels were often carrying war supplies so this
rather gentlemanly policy ended and any ships
discovered in the war zones were liable to be sunk
without warning. Submarines now used torpedoes,
remaining submerged and aiming through a
periscope from a distance of up to 2500m. To
disguise a moving ship presented a different
problem to hiding a stationary object like a
building or a field gun which could be painted to
match the background. With a warship in variable
light and the constantly changing sea and sky as a
background conventional camouflage was impossible.

uss 'West Mohemot' in dock

Artists and designers in France and America were
working on this problem and coming up with various
ideas for disguise based on animal camouflage,
counter shading, etc.

In this country in early 1917 a Royal Navy officer,
Norman Wilkinson, who was also an academic marine
painter, came up with a solution. Instead of trying
to hide the ship against its background he proposed
that its visible shape be 'confused' by using
irregular geometric patterns, thus 'dazzling' any
submarine gunner so that he could not be sure
about the target's true course, size or distance
as he tried quickly to aim his torpedo. Because
the torpedo had to be fired in front of the ship,
to the position it would reach by the time the
weapon struck, it was essential that the ship's
speed was accurately judged by the marksman on the
submarine.

Wilkinson's disruptive camouflage made this
judgment very difficult. The ship could be seen
clearly but which way was it sailing? How fast was
it travelling? Was it going left or right?

It was an effective solution and soon, as a test, 50 troopships were painted with the 'Dazzle' designs. Wilkinson himself was put in charge of the newly-formed Camouflage Section in a basement studio at the Royal Academy where designs were tried out on scale model ships.

Most contemporary photos of the warships are in black and white so it's easy to forget how colourfully striking they must have looked.

The art dealer Rene Gimpel wrote:
'(A dazzle painted ship) was like an enormous cubist painting with great sheets of ultramarine blue, black and green, sometimes parallel but more often with sharp corners cleaving into one another...'

Among the officers who supervised the painting at the docks from the designs worked out at the RA was the artist Edward Wadsworth and he made several paintings and some beautiful woodcuts based on 'Dazzle' ships in harbour and dry dock.

By the end of June 1918 2,300 British ships had been painted and it must have been an incredible sight to see a mass of these camouflaged ships in harbour. Here's an account by Hugh Hurst in 1919 from *International Studio*:

'Those who were not fortunate to see the docks at one of our great ports during the war may imagine the arrival of a convoy – or, as frequently occurred, two at a time – of these painted ships, and the many miles of docks crowded with vessels of all sorts...each resplendent with bright-hued patterns, up-to-date designs of stripes in black and white or pale blue and deep ultramarine, and earlier designs of curves, patches and semicircles. Take all these, huddle them together in what appears

'Drydocked for Scaling and Painting'
Edward Wadsworth - woodcut 1918

to be a hopeless confusion, but which in reality
is perfect order, bow and stern pointing in all
directions, mix in a little sunshine, add the varied
and sparkling reflections, stir the hotchpotch up
with smoke, life and incessant movement, and it
can safely be said that the word "dazzle" is not
far from the mark.'

To take from the earth

a handful of colour

Just recently I've been working on a series of pastels which I've called *The Red Tent*. It's a simple image about hope, a stylised tent shape against a white background.

The idea came after reading an account of an arctic tragedy in May 1928 when the airship *Italia* came down in a storm on an expedition to the North Pole. Half the crew were marooned in the wreckage of the gondola as, weighed down by ice, the airship lost altitude and crashed near the pole. The cabin detached itself on impact and the rest of the men were lost, carried away clinging to the envelope of the balloon as, now much lighter, it rose up and disappeared into the blizzard. To increase the likelihood of being spotted by rescuers searching for them the survivors erected a tarpaulin tent for shelter and coloured it bright red, using dye from marker bombs in the debris. The few survivors on the ice were eventually rescued but tragically the famous arctic explorer Roald Amundsen died in one of the search parties out hunting for them.

After I began working on the pastels I found an interesting painting that Kitaj made in 1964, full of shadowy figures, called *Dismantling the Red Tent* which seemed at first sight to be directly related to, or at least influenced by, the *Italia* story. Kitaj's own account of 'this little mystery picture' does reference the tent as a beacon of hope and also the element of politics is there but into his story he brings regicide – the assassination of President Kennedy:

The Red Tent was a beacon used by polar explorers in the wastes ... coming into the warm from the cold I take To be one of the meanings of art, the political men in my picture (some hollow, some not) hover about The Red Tent for warmth after a regicide, the perpetual play of governance by consent in which Hannah Arendt called 'the public space.'

Kitaj — Dismantling the Red Tent

I was really intrigued by this painting which I've only seen in reproduction (the original is in the LA County Museum), but I don't think, without finding Kitaj's own explanation, I would have understood what he intended it to be about.

Prior to seeing those notes my reading of the image, taking the title as a clue, was that the 'dismantling' had something to do with the American desire to take apart (bring down) the Soviet Union during that tense period of the Cold War.

If that was the case, then why include the etching
by Alphonse Legros of the old, bent peasant on
the road collaged to the picture, top left? How
did that fit in with my idea of the defeat of
communism? Unfortunately I was way off the mark
anyway, the painting turns out not to be about
the overthrow of the Russian State at all.
But it obviously had a meaning or story of sorts
and he had after all called it himself a 'mystery
painting', and mysteries surely have solutions?
Part of Kitaj's gloss on the picture (he called
these explanations 'Prefaces'), written twenty
years after the work was painted, says:

I've been told by experts that
democracy, about two centuries
old and experienced by only a
tiny minority of people, may have
been an historical accident whose
days look numbered. As often as
that thought scares me, another
similar intelligence keeps
sneaking up on me, about our own
— that this art, with which you
and I try to mean something, and
about which so few of us agree, for
all its modern attractiveness, seems
(to me any way) a frail exercise,
like democracy itself, practised
almost hopelessly at the far
margins of a vast world bent on
the destruction of democracy by
men without art."

I have liked Kitaj's work since the first time I saw it properly in 1963. His one-man show was on at Marlborough New London and my art teacher, Eric Taylor, (we remained friends until he died a few years ago) advised his small class of four sixth-formers to go to the gallery to see what he called 'the most interesting exhibition in London'.

I don't remember worrying about the meaning of the pictures then because I think first and foremost I was impressed by Kitaj's technical skill – he seemed to me such a good draughtsman and the pictures energetic and confident – but the question was there, if unrecognised by me at the time, as to what the paintings were fully about, what stories or references were hidden within the work? How could one begin to fathom things out and is it a good or a bad thing for a work of art to be dependent or reliant on scholarly knowledge?

Above me on the bookshelf, as I write, I notice Kitaj frowning down at me disapprovingly from a book jacket for mentioning this subject again.

In bringing up this question of meaning - which certainly doesn't apply only to Kitaj - I don't want to sound like any of the critics who attacked him so savagely, during his Tate retrospective in 1994, for what they saw as his over-reliance on literary sources and explanations. That concerted attack on him is still shocking if you read it today.

Plenty of work throughout the history of western art has depended on literary underpinning by a story or myth. What do you think about this question of a work becoming too dependent on a mass of scholarly footnotes or arcane references for its meaning? Maybe Kitaj began to answer the question from his own point of view with his phrase 'some books have pictures and some pictures have books', which he wrote around the same time that *Dismantling the Red Tent* was painted.

My *Red Tent* is much less of a puzzle in its structure and allusions than Kitaj's painting and no doubt suffers in this direct comparison but I thought you might be interested to see the two together. Perhaps even with this simple image you need to know the *Italia* story – although that knowledge brings with it the danger of turning the image into an illustration of the story which wasn't my intention.

I like the direct idea of this red geometric shape, drawing attention to itself and signifying hope in a sea of whiteness. The very opposite of hiding in plain view.

with love from us all

John.

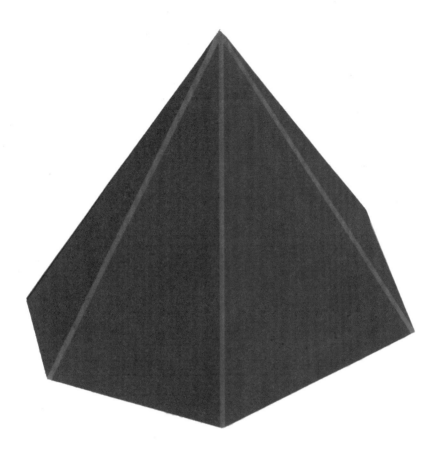

ITALIA

'Mean something! You and I, mean something! Ah, that's a good one!'
Samuel Beckett quoted by R. B. Kitaj in notes on his painting *Dismantling the Red Tent*

Last weekend it snowed quite hard overnight and the low daily temperatures mean that the covering of snow has lingered on. Walking my usual route around the wood today surrounded by white fields I could see evidence of animals everywhere, thousands of small footprints (there's a Suffolk dialect word for them, *feetings*) but no creatures in sight, frightened away probably, if they had been nearby, by the sound of my boots compacting the frozen snow. It was impossible to walk silently and my footsteps carried across the open ground and into the darkness of the wood. As the footpath crossed the fields I did have the luck to see a barn owl. I spotted him some way off and waited, quite still on the open path willing him to come towards me, while he patrolled the ditch around the edge of the field. Gradually he came nearer to the spot where I stood. He was only feet away, almost it felt, close enough to touch, when his eyes flicked up from searching the ground and noticed me. A sharp change of direction and he was silently away across the snow to carry on hunting in private.

For some reason Livorno was in my mind, perhaps because I'd been thinking about your letter and your connection with the city, Modigliani's birthplace, and I had the vague recollection that your book *G* begins there. When I got home I checked and there it was, Livorno, in the second line. Holding the book again reminded me of what a good job Richard Hollis had made of the design – the jacket still looks striking and distinctive. Later editions unfortunately didn't fair so well. There's another small connection with Livorno and *Bento's Sketchbook* that I remember. Modigliani's mother claimed Spinoza as one of her family's Jewish ancestors, through a blood line from the philosopher's younger brother. I'm not sure where I read that but I hope, for connectivity, it's true.

I mentioned that Sunday lunch in the early 90s with Pru Clough and you said you couldn't find a photo of her. Well here is a picture from that day that my friends have unearthed, it was in February, near Valentine's Day, we think. Perhaps that way of holding her hand and the cigarette is familiar to you? Did you ever do any drawings of each other?

I called in to see Derrick and Sally (Greaves) the other day on my way back from Norwich. He had some new work on the go that I was keen to see and also I wanted to take a photo of Pru's work-glove collage. I discovered that my memory had played a trick on me and there wasn't a pair, just one glove with a large nail fixing it to the backboard – perhaps she'd gone back later to retrieve it from the Goods Yard?

Up until the mid-90s most of my graphic work, if that is the right word, took the form of books and prints made, mainly at Circle Press, between times when I wasn't filming. It was a good arrangement as long as the gap between camerawork and directing jobs didn't get too long and the money too thin.

I was thinking about this work balance the other day as I watched the light changing in my studio. At this time of the year the sun is at such a low angle that it comes skating straight in and, because

of the strong shadows, makes it difficult to work unless the sunlight is softened with tracing paper over the windows. I watched the shadows slowly crossing my drawing board as the sun began to go down. When I turned the overhead lights on the atmosphere in the space changed again and I realised that for most of my working life I've been thinking about light, collecting the memories of how light falls in a room or on a face. Sometimes it was a very conscious activity as when considering and planning how to light a particular scene for a drama. But mostly it was something I'd trained myself to do automatically – remembering a pleasing or unusual combination of light; how tungsten light mixed with daylight in a room; how soft light wrapped itself around an object; how a room could be animated by shadows from action outside the frame. I stored these effects in my memory for later, for the time they might come in useful. The film lighting I enjoyed doing most was the kind that didn't draw attention to itself, where the scene or the portrait appeared not to be lit at all except by natural light.

Now, instead of light, I work mostly with paper and coloured pastels, a medium I took up after I came back from a trip to Australia in 2000. I'd been invited to make a print at the art school in Canberra and wanting to try to come to the subject afresh I didn't take any visual material with me from home. I did take in my notebook a quotation from the Australian architect Glenn Murcutt, a simple instruction, originating I think from an observation by Thoreau, so that buildings might sit harmoniously in the landscape:

'Take a handful of earth at your feet and paint your house that colour'

That phrase took me to the beginnings of an idea for the print. Flying for hours on end over the countryside and seeing the colouring of red iron oxide and yellow ochre in the expanses of the landscape I decided to use these earth colours, which I found so beautiful, for my Australian print.

On my first day in Canberra (I'd been in Perth for the previous week) everywhere in the city was fairly empty because people were sitting at home watching the Sydney Olympics on TV. That morning, to push the travelling out of my head, I went to look around the National Gallery. On the way back to my flat in the art school I picked up, on the banks of the lake outside the gallery, another element I thought might help me to begin next day, a bunch of dried gum tree leaves. I had some great practical help from the team in the print workshop and we finished the edition in a few days before I headed back to London.

In the middle of this letter I've made a version of that print for you, with pastel providing the colours instead of the original earth pigments.

I brought some bags of coloured earth home with me but in the studio found the powder very difficult to control – it went everywhere and it was then that I turned to pastel. I could match any of the earth colours with a pastel and they were much easier to handle than the raw powder.

As I got more technically used to working with pastel I increased my colour range from those initial earth pigments and also began to make small wooden constructions. Sometimes the construction came first, sometimes the pastel on paper. The form of the work looked to European Constructivism but I tried to see if I could introduce the idea of changing viewpoints and depth to the works on paper, something I could do with a 3D construction just by moving the position of my head. These changes in my work came in part from the discovery of 'Dazzle' Camouflage at the Imperial War Museum in London. This was the Navy's practical solution, introduced towards the end of World War One and used well into the Second, of disguising ships at sea with disruptive patterning to confuse the eye – a way to hide them in plain view.

During the period from March to December 1917 German submarines sank on average more than 23 Allied ships each week, a total of over 900 ships.

At the beginning of the war when a U-boat attacked an enemy ship the submarine would surface, making it vulnerable to attack, and fire on the ship with it's deck-mounted cannon. If the target was an unarmed merchant ship, the submarine would pull alongside, evacuate everyone on board into the lifeboats before sinking the ship. Merchant vessels were often carrying war supplies so this rather gentlemanly policy ended and any ships discovered in the war zones were liable to be sunk without warning. Submarines now used torpedoes, remaining submerged and aiming through a periscope from a distance of up to 2,500m. To disguise a moving ship presented a different problem to hiding a stationary object like a building or a field gun which could be painted to match the background. With a warship in variable light and the constantly changing sea and sky as a background conventional camouflage was impossible.

Artists and designers in France and America were working on this problem and coming up with various ideas for disguise based on animal camouflage, counter shading, etc. In this country in early 1917 a Royal Navy officer, Norman Wilkinson, who was also an academic marine painter, came up with a solution. Instead of trying to hide the ship against its background he proposed that its visible shape be 'confused' by using irregular geometric patterns, thus 'dazzling' any submarine gunner so that he could not be sure about the target's true course, size or distance as he tried quickly to aim his torpedo. Because the torpedo had to be fired in front of the ship, to the position it would reach by the time the weapon struck, it was essential that the ship's speed was accurately judged by the marksman on the submarine.

Wilkinson's disruptive camouflage made this judgment very difficult. The ship could be seen clearly but which way was it sailing? How fast was it travelling? Was it going left or right? It was an effective solution and soon, as a test, 50 troopships were painted with the 'Dazzle' designs. Wilkinson himself was put in charge of the newly-formed Camouflage Section in a basement studio at the Royal Academy where designs were tried out on scale model ships.

Most contemporary photos of the warships are in black and white so it's easy to forget how colourfully striking they must have looked.
The art dealer Rene Gimpel wrote:
'(A dazzle painted ship) was like an enormous cubist painting with great sheets of ultramarine blue, black and green, sometimes

parallel but more often with sharp corners cleaving into one another...'

Among the officers who supervised the painting at the docks from the designs worked out at the RA was the artist Edward Wadsworth and he made several paintings and some beautiful woodcuts based on 'Dazzle' ships in harbour and dry dock.

By the end of June 1918 2,300 British ships had been painted and it must have been an incredible sight to see a mass of these camouflaged ships in harbour. Here's an account by Hugh Hurst in 1919 from *International Studio*:

'Those who were not fortunate to see the docks at one of our great ports during the war may imagine the arrival of a convoy – or, as frequently occurred, two at a time – of these painted ships, and the many miles of docks crowded with vessels of all sorts ...each resplendent with bright-hued patterns, up-to-date designs of stripes in black and white or pale blue and deep ultramarine, and earlier designs of curves, patches and semicircles. Take all these, huddle them together in what appears to be a hopeless confusion, but which in reality is perfect order, bow and stern pointing in all directions, mix in a little sunshine, add the varied and sparkling reflections, stir the hotchpotch up with smoke, life and incessant movement, and it can safely be said that the word "dazzle" is not far from the mark.'

Just recently I've been working on a series of pastels which I've called *The Red Tent*. It's a simple image about hope, a stylised tent shape against a white background.

The idea came after reading an account of an arctic tragedy in May 1928 when the airship *Italia* came down in a storm on an expedition to the North Pole. Half the crew were marooned in the wreckage of the gondola as, weighed down by ice, the airship lost altitude and crashed near the pole. The cabin detached itself on impact and the rest of the men were lost, carried away clinging to the envelope of the balloon as, now much lighter, it rose up and disappeared into the blizzard. To increase the likelihood of being spotted by rescuers searching for them the survivors erected a tarpaulin tent for shelter and coloured it bright red, using dye from marker bombs in the debris. The few survivors on the ice were eventually rescued but tragically the famous arctic explorer Roald Amundsen died in one of the search parties out hunting for them.

After I began working on the pastels I found an interesting painting that Kitaj made in 1964, full of shadowy figures, called *Dismantling the Red Tent* which seemed at first sight to be directly related to, or at least influenced by, the *Italia* story. Kitaj's own account of 'this little mystery picture' does reference the tent as a beacon of hope and also the element of politics is there but into his story he brings regicide – the assassination of President Kennedy:

'The Red Tent was a beacon used by polar explorers in the wastes ... Coming in to warm from the cold I take to be one of the meanings of art, the political men in my picture (some hollow, some not) hover about the Red Tent for warmth after a regicide, a perpetual play of governance by consent in which Hannah Arendt called "the public space".'

I was really intrigued by this painting which I've only seen in reproduction (the original is in the LA County Museum), but I don't think, without finding Kitaj's own explanation I would have understood what he intended it to be about.

Prior to seeing those notes my reading of the image, taking the title as a clue, was that the 'dismantling' had something to do with the American desire to take apart (bring down) the Soviet Union during that tense period of the Cold War. If that was the case, then why include the etching by Alphonse Legros of the old, bent peasant on the road collaged to the picture, top left? How did that fit in with my idea of the defeat of communism? Unfortunately I was way off the mark anyway, the painting turns out not to be about the overthrow of the Russian State at all. But it obviously had a meaning or story of sorts and he had after all called it himself a 'mystery painting', and mysteries surely have solutions? Part of Kitaj's gloss on the picture (he called these explanations 'Prefaces'), written twenty years after the work was painted, says:

'I've been told by experts that democracy, about two centuries old and experienced by only a tiny minority of people, may have been an historical accident whose days look numbered. As often as that thought scares me, another, similar intelligence keeps sneaking up on me, about our art – that this art, with which you and I try to mean something, and about which so few of us agree, for all its modern attractiveness, seems (to me anyway) a frail exercise, like democracy itself, practiced almost hopelessly at the far margins of a vast world bent on the destruction of democracy by Men Without Art.'

I have liked Kitaj's work since the first time I saw it properly in 1963. His one-man show was on at Marlborough New London and my art teacher, Eric Taylor, (we remained friends until he died a few years ago) advised his small class of four sixth-formers to go to the gallery to see what he called 'the most interesting exhibition in London'.

I don't remember worrying about the meaning of the pictures then because I think first and foremost I was impressed by Kitaj's technical skill – he seemed to me such a good draughtsman and the pictures energetic and confident – but the question was there, if unrecognised by me at the time, as to what the paintings were fully about, what stories or references were hidden within the work? How could one begin to fathom things out and is it a good or a bad thing for a work of art to be dependent or reliant on scholarly knowledge?
Above me on the bookshelf, as I write, I notice Kitaj frowning down at me disapprovingly from a book jacket for mentioning this subject again.

In bringing up this question of meaning – which certainly doesn't apply only to Kitaj – I don't want to sound like any of the critics who attacked him so savagely, during his Tate retrospective in 1994, for what they saw as his over-reliance on literary sources and explanations. That concerted attack on him is still shocking if you read it today.

Plenty of work throughout the history of western art has depended on literary underpinning by a story or myth. What do you think about this question of a work becoming too dependent on a mass of scholarly footnotes or arcane references for its meaning? Maybe Kitaj began to answer the question from his own point of view with his phrase 'some books have pictures and some pictures have books' which he wrote around the same time that *Dismantling the Red Tent* was painted.

My *Red Tent* is much less of a puzzle in its structure and allusions than Kitaj's painting and no doubt suffers in this direct comparison but I thought you might be interested to see the two together. Perhaps even with this simple image you need to know the *Italia* story – although that knowledge brings with it the danger of turning the image into an illustration of the story which wasn't my intention.

I like the direct idea of this red geometric shape, drawing attention to itself and signifying hope in a sea of whiteness. The very opposite of hiding in plain view.

With love from us all
John

from John Berger May 2012

12/5/12.

Dear John,

I like the Canberra print a
lot. It's very physical. ~~You~~ One senses
the earthiness of the two earth colours which
your plane flew over. One hears the
sound the dried gum-tree leaves make
when they are stirred by ~~the~~ a breeze.
And because of this physicality, the whole
image, with its three parts, comes within
touching distance, like the barn-owl
~~you~~ you met in the snow.

And talking of touching distance,
thank you for the photo of Pru. You ask
me if I recognise something in the way
she's holding her hands. Yes, I do.
Her hands were deeply characteristic of
her. She had the hands of a
full-time gardener. Though in fact
she never, insofar as I know,
gardened. Her field of vision was her
garden. And her studio was somehow
like a garden-shed with garden tools.
We sat on the grass together, our backs
to a fence.

2.

The print of the red tent. The perspective you found for drawing the tent is very tent-like. And the white paper for the snow is O.K. But for it to acquire physicality — and not remain the diagram of an idea —) think a third element is needed.) don't know what. Perhaps something to do with ice? A cloud? There is the third element of the lettering and the word Italia — but this remains an abstract (and unless you know the story) mystifying reference. No more. A third physical element is needed) reckon.

And this brings me round to what you say about Kitay. His <u>Dismantling the Red Tent</u> lacks for me any physical authority or authenticity. Its an image of echoes not substances. It exists like a noise, not an object or a body. He has very little tactile sense. And so <u>information</u> (prophetic concerning the digital which was to come) takes over from the manual. And this is perhaps why he is accused of being a wind-bag. To put it another way, he's placeless. This is not to put him down, it's simply to explain why ~~to~~ I never got close to his work. Maybe my limitation?

What is the secret of the art of ∧ painting, as distinct from photography or video or film? It has little ∧ ~~nothing~~ to do with iconography or symbolism. It has to do with its capacity to embody, to bring within touching distance ∧ something which is intangible and not there. It has many ways of doing this and all of them play with tangibility. Its' not by chance ~~that~~ the human hand is there as a witness when painting began (Chauvet) in the caves.

Camouflage, as your dazzle-ships so strikingly ~~d.~~ demonstrate, confuses the identity, placing, destination of real substantial things. And it does this with paint and colours. The art of painting does the opposite. It gives a body and an identity and a destination to some being or object or place which, in reality, is not there. It does this of course with the "collaboration" of its spectators, and this collaboration is possible because of their knowledge and their beliefs but also because of their experience and memories of touch. All painting — even the most abstract — is involved in making the intangible tangible.

Was this the message of your barn-owl

I embrace you and

Geneviève and Alice

John

Dear John

I like the Canberra print a lot. It's very physical. One senses the earthiness of the two earth colours which your plane flew over. One hears the sound the dried gum tree leaves make when they are stirred by a breeze. And because of this physicality, the whole image, with its three parts, comes within touching distance, like the barn owl you met in the snow.

And talking of touching distance, thank you for the photo of Pru. You ask me if I recognise something in the way she's holding her hands? Yes, I do. Her hands were deeply characteristic of her. She had the hands of a full-time gardener. Though in fact she never, insofar as I know, gardened. Her field of vision was her garden. And her studio was somehow like a garden-shed with garden tools. We sat on the grass together, our backs to a fence.

The print of the red tent. The perspective you found for drawing the tent is very tent-like. The white paper for the snow is OK. But for it to acquire physicality – and not remain the diagram of an idea – I think a third element is needed. I don't know what. Perhaps something to do with ice? A cloud? There is the third element of the lettering and the word Italia – but this remains an abstract (and unless you know the story) mystifying reference. No more. A third physical element is needed I reckon.

And this brings me round to what you say about Kitaj. His *Dismantling the Red Tent* lacks for me any physical authority or authenticity. It's an image of echoes not substances. It exists like a noise, not an object or a body. He has very little tactile sense. And so information (prophetic concerning the digital which was to come) takes over from the manual. And this is perhaps why he is accused of being a wind-bag. To put it another way, he's placeless. This is not to put him down, it's simply to explain why I never got close to his work. Maybe my limitation?

What is the secret of the art of painting, as distinct from photography or video or film? It has little to do with iconography or symbolism. It has to do with its capacity to embody, to bring within touching distance something which is intangible and not there. It has many ways of doing this and all of them play with intangibility. It's not by chance that the human hand is there as a witness when painting began (Chauvet) in the caves.

Camouflage, as your dazzle-ships so strikingly demonstrate, confuses the identity, placing, destination of real substantial things. And it does this with paint and colours. The art of painting does the opposite. It gives a body an identity and a destination to some being or object which, in reality, is not there. It does this of course with the 'collaboration' of its spectators, and this collaboration is possible because of their knowledge and their beliefs but also because of their experience and memories of touch. All painting – even the most abstract – is involved in making the intangible tangible.
Was this the message of your barn-owl?

I embrace you and Genevieve and Alice
John

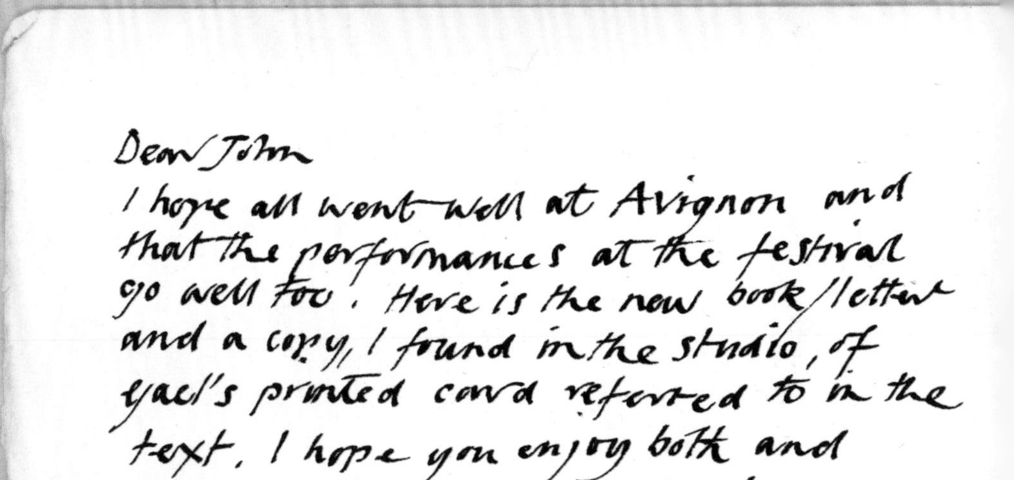

Dear John

I hope all went well at Avignon and that the performances at the festival go well too. Here is the new book/letter and a copy, I found in the studio, of Gael's printed card referred to in the text. I hope you enjoy both and look forward to hearing from you soon.

Love John

Text: Gael Turnbull   Print: John Christie   Circle Press 1982

The density of certain stars is so slight

that on earth they would be an almost perfect vacuum

and yet their presence can be clearly perceived

without the aid of any instrument

from the other side of the universe

with one glance of the human eye.

from John Christie June 2012

Looking on Glass

I would say that what interests me about the theatre is that no reply is possible. When the curtain falls you leave. A work of art should have this quality of not admitting a reply.

Juan Muñoz

Dear John

A strange, magical thing happened a few weeks ago when Iona and David were staying for the weekend. The weather was behaving itself for once this wet summer and after lunch we asked Alice to play for us. The windows and doors were open and we could hear the sound of her flute as we stood outside on the terrace listening to the music and looking across the fields towards the wood. Gradually six fallow deer emerged from the trees and stood looking across at us. They were about 400 metres away and standing quite still, watching us watching them and listening too, or so it seemed. When the music stopped they appeared to lose interest in us and began eating and moving slowly along the tree line until one by one they disappeared back into the wood. Once they'd gone Alice began playing again and slowly the deer emerged from the wood once more and stood staring fixedly across at us, ears pricked. I didn't take a photo at the time because I was fascinated by what I was seeing. We haven't tried it again, better to keep the memory of that moment intact.

I haven't done anything further to the *Red Tent* pastel because I realised, after I sent it to you, that it wasn't a separate image and did need to remain with the story to make sense, so your observation that it was 'the diagram of an idea' was correct. Perhaps it is, in the end, no more than an illustration to the story. It could also be, it seems to me now, the logo for a company selling clothes or even camping equipment or the jacket image for a book about the doomed expedition. This question of 'illustration' versus 'art' is a tricky one. Perhaps the difference lies in the intention or purpose of the image. What I was trying to make was a self-contained symbol of hope not an illustration but as you have to know the story for that to work, it rather failed on that level.

A month or so ago Lali asked me, together with a few others, to write something to go with Eugenia Balcell's new work 'Universe', a large, fragile globe turning slowly in a dark space and made up of six or eight semi-transparent segments onto which are projected film fragments of the physical world and the heavens. I thought about it for a few weeks but felt rather intimidated, not by Eugenia's work but by the word 'universe'. Hoping it would be enough I emailed Lali a text I had by Gael Turnbull, a dear friend who died a few years ago, which seemed to quietly fit the brief. It had been sent to me 30-odd years ago, a poem for a printed card:

The density of certain stars is so slight
that on earth they would be an almost perfect
* vacuum*
and yet their presence can be clearly perceived
without the aid of any instrument
from the other side of the universe
with one glance of the human eye.

When we lived in London the stars in the night sky were often obscured by light pollution from the city and it was always a shock to see the quantity of stars visible to the naked eye when away from built-up areas, especially when I travelled to remote mountain and desert areas. You wrote in your story *Time of the Cosmonauts* how after a hard days work, when the Italian woodcutters sat around the fire, the sight of the stars in the night sky provoked stories and songs. One place I experienced this was on a trip to Russia in 1992.

I was there to make a travel film, firstly in Moscow and St. Petersburg then in the more impoverished satellite states in the far south. There were five of us in the team and we flew from Moscow to Tashkent, visiting first Samarkand and then Bukhara in Uzbekistan. In Samarkand I remember filming Tamerlane's dusty tomb and the ruins of the astronomer Ulugh Beg's observatory. Built in the 15th century all that remains of the observatory is the underground stone channel of the great sextant, a small section of the original 40m diameter mechanical instrument used to measure and map the heavens. Without the aid of telescopes Ulugh Beg compiled a catalogue of almost 1000 stars and managed to calculate the length of a year, to within less than half a minute, using the sextant. I also remember my hotel room in Samarkand where no tap could be turned off properly so that the basin, toilet and shower ran noisily all night – we nicknamed it the 'Niagara Suite'.

We travelled too through mile upon mile of cotton fields before crossing the border into Tajikistan. We were heading to a section of the Great Silk Road leading to the Marguzor Lakes where, off the main highway and a day's journey into the mountains, we came to the famous string of seven large lakes along the ancient trade route. Instead of camels our transport was a battered four-wheel drive bus whose shot suspension transmitted every judder and jolt from the rocks and potholes along the track. It was a slow journey made longer by stopping every now and then to film in the tiny villages that we passed through. This 20th-century version of the Silk Road followed the river that connected the lakes. We skirted the first two until, after dark, we reached our overnight stop just before the third lake. The tents were pitched on some flat ground beside the river and for a while, after we'd eaten, our local guide sang for us, haunting shepherd's songs that hung in the night air above the fire; they turned out, when translated, to be mostly about love and sheep (sometimes, if the translation was correct, about both at the same time).

Everyone was tired and an early night was necessary as we had a climb of over 2500 metres to the mountain top before us the next day. It was cold and I lay there in my sleeping bag wondering if, even with my previous experience in the 'Niagara Suite' I'd be able to sleep at all with the sounds of the river in my ears. The night sky was filled with stars and you could understand how, when men tried to explain the visible universe, they imagined the darkness as a vast circular sphere around the Earth, pierced by holes, letting in light from beyond.

The dramatic night sky for some reason brought the verse, remembered from my school days, of a hymn by George Herbert into my head:

A man that looks on glass,
On it may stay his eye;
Or if he pleaseth, through it pass,
And then the heavens espy.

The complete poem, which is full of references to alchemy, was published a year after Herbert's death in 1633, and much later set to music as a hymn ('Teach me my God and King'). Although the meaning now seems fairly straightforward as a young boy I didn't understand what this verse was about and my school music teacher tried to explain it by using the simple image of glass in a window on which you could focus your gaze or with imagination look through the glass and see the wonders of the wider world beyond. It could also mean 'glass' as in 'looking-glass' or mirror, a plea to look through your own self to see the larger perspective or, in religious terms, the Kingdom of Heaven.

Looking up I found I had no sense of perspective, the stars seemed to all be the same distance from me making me feel like the focus of the things I was seeing. This is not to describe a mystical experience, rather a confusing visual sensation. In an essay on Vladimir Tatlin's work Margit Rowell talks about a similar effect:

'In conventional Western art perspective may be defined in terms of a pyramid of space. The tip of the pyramid is at the furthest point of depth, behind the object and therefore penetrates the wall. In the icon the tip is in front of the object, in the viewer's eye, and the base of the pyramid is the wall's surface. Thus the icon's inverse perspective projected the object and its meaning into the viewers actual space, the space of existential experience.'

Confronted with the bewildering mass of stars above my head I seemed to be experiencing something like this 'icon perspective' when, turning slightly, I noticed for the first time that a whole section of the sky was black and empty.

I woke early next morning, the air was freezing and the flow of the river noisier than ever. The tent was in deep shadow because just the other side of the rushing water, less than 50m away, the sheer wall of the mountain, invisible in the darkness of the previous night, rose vertically blocking out the sun, blocking out half the sky.

After breakfast we started the five-hour ascent to the top from where I could photograph four of the seven lakes stretching off into the far distance, different blues against the dusty brown of the mountains. I was an observer again, back behind the glass.

Here are a couple of photos from that trip into the mountains. Over the page the view from the top that day showing two of the lakes in the valley and, below, me cooling my feet in the shallows after we got back to camp.

In the Sainsbury collection the other day I had a
moment where I felt quite low. I'm very familiar
with the work on show there now and perhaps for
that reason I was looking for something different,
something I hadn't noticed before. It's difficult
with a fixed collection for works to take you by
surprise and it seemed that at that moment some of
the life had gone out of certain of the pieces. For
instance an Epstein head of a sleeping baby and a
soapstone head from Sierra Leone, both quite near
each other in the displays, took on the appearance
of severed heads with their cleanly cut necks and
closed eyes. A visual impression I remember you
talking about in the past.

Jacob Epstein 'Baby Asleep' 1902-04

Male Head — Sierra Leone 15/16th c

Of course the display captions nearby didn't mention anything about death or severed heads and I felt disappointed with myself for viewing them in that way. Not far away I found a beautiful, finely carved torso from Cambodia. It is not very big, only 43cm high, and probably if you could put both hands round her waist you'd be able to touch your thumb and finger tips together. No head but full of life — she cheered me up.

With Love from us all
John

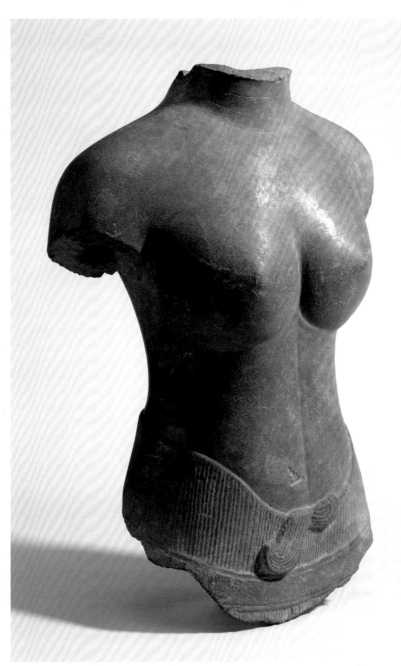

Female Torso — Cambodia 11th c

Dear John

I hope all went well at Avignon and that the performances at the
festival go well too. Here is the new book/letter and a copy,
I found in the studio, of Gael's printed card referred to in the text.
I hope you enjoy both and look forward to hearing from you soon.
Love John

'I would say that what interests me about the theatre is that no
reply is possible. When the curtain falls you leave. A work of art
should have this quality of not admitting a reply.'
Juan Muñoz

Dear John

A strange, magical thing happened a few weeks ago when Iona
and David (Heath) were staying for the weekend. The weather
was behaving itself for once this wet summer and after lunch we
asked Alice to play for us. The windows and doors were open and
we could hear the sound of her flute as we stood outside on the
terrace listening to the music and looking across the fields towards
the wood. Gradually six fallow deer emerged from the trees and
stood looking across at us. They were about 400 metres away and
standing quite still, watching us watching them and listening too, or
so it seemed. When the music stopped they appeared to lose
interest in us and began eating and moving slowly along the tree
line until one by one they disappeared back into the wood. Once
they'd gone Alice began playing again and slowly the deer
emerged from the wood once more and stood staring fixedly
across at us, ears pricked. I didn't take a photo at the time because
I was fascinated by what I was seeing. We haven't tried it again,
better to keep the memory of that moment intact.

I haven't done anything further to the *Red Tent* pastel because
I realised, after I sent it to you, that it wasn't a separate image but
needed to remain with the story to make sense, so your observation
that it was 'the diagram of an idea' was correct. Perhaps it is, in the
end, no more than an illustration of part of the story. It could be,
it seems to me now, the logo for a company selling clothes or
even camping equipment or the jacket image for a book about
the failed expedition. This question of 'illustration' versus 'art' is a
tricky one. Perhaps the difference lies in the intention or purpose
of the image. What I was trying to make was a self-contained
symbol of hope not an illustration but as you have to know the
story for that to work, it rather failed on that level.

A month or so ago Lali (Bosch) asked me, together with a few
others, to write something to go with Eugenia Balcell's new work
'Universe', a large, fragile globe turning slowly in a dark space and
made up of six or eight semi-transparent segments onto which
are projected film fragments of the physical world and the heavens.
I thought about it for a few weeks but felt rather intimidated, not
by Eugenia's work but by the word 'universe'. Hoping it would be
enough I emailed Lali a text I had by Gael Turnbull, a dear friend
who died a few years ago, which seemed to quietly fit the brief.
It had been sent to me 30-odd years ago, a poem for a printed
card:

The density of certain stars is so slight
that on earth they would be an almost perfect vacuum
and yet their presence can be clearly perceived
without the aid of any instrument
from the other side of the universe
with one glance of the human eye.

When we lived in London the stars in the night sky were often
obscured by light pollution from the city and it was always a
shock to see the quantity of stars visible to the naked eye when
away from built-up areas, especially when I travelled to remote
mountain and desert areas. You wrote in your story *Time of the
Cosmonauts* how after a hard days work, when the Italian woodcutters sat around the fire, the sight of the stars in the night sky
provoked stories and songs. One place I experienced this was on
a trip to Russia in 1992.

I was there to make a travel film, firstly in Moscow and St. Petersburg
then in the more impoverished satellite states in the far south.
There were five of us in the team and we flew from Moscow to
Tashkent, visiting first Samarkand and then Bukhara in Uzbekistan.
In Samarkand I remember filming Tamerlane's dusty tomb and the
ruins of the astronomer Ulugh Beg's observatory. Built in the 15th
century all that remains of the observatory is the underground
stone channel of the great sextant, a small section of the original
40m diameter mechanical instrument used to measure and map
the heavens. Without the aid of telescopes Ulugh Beg compiled
a catalogue of almost 1000 stars and managed to calculate the
length of a year, to within less than half a minute, using the sextant.
I also remember my hotel room in Samarkand where no tap
could be turned off properly so that the basin, toilet and shower
ran noisily all night – we nicknamed it the 'Niagara Suite'.

We travelled too through mile upon mile of cotton fields before
crossing the border into Tajikistan. We were heading to a section
of the Great Silk Road leading to the Marguzor Lakes where, off
the main highway and a day's journey into the mountains, we
came to the famous string of seven large lakes along the ancient
trade route. Instead of camels our transport was a battered four-
wheel drive bus whose shot suspension transmitted every judder
and jolt from the rocks and potholes along the track. It was a slow
journey made longer by stopping every now and then to film in
the tiny villages that we passed through. This 20th-century version
of the Silk Road followed the river that connected the lakes. We
skirted the first two until, after dark, we reached our overnight
stop just before the third lake. The tents were pitched on some
flat ground beside the river and for a while, after we'd eaten, our
local guide sang for us, haunting shepherd's songs that hung in the
night air above the fire; they turned out, when translated, to be
mostly about love and sheep (sometimes, if the translation was
correct, about both at the same time).

Everyone was tired and an early night was necessary as we had
a climb of over 2500 metres to the mountain top before us the
next day. It was cold and I lay there in my sleeping bag wondering
if, even with my previous experience in the 'Niagara Suite' I'd be
able to sleep at all with the sounds of the river in my ears. The
night sky was filled with stars and you could understand how,
when men tried to explain the visible universe, they imagined the
darkness as a vast circular sphere around the Earth, pierced by

holes, letting in light from beyond. The dramatic night sky for some reason brought the verse, remembered from my school days, of a hymn by George Herbert into my head:

A man that looks on glass,
On it may stay his eye;
Or if he pleaseth, through it pass,
And then the heavens espy.

The complete poem, which is full of references to alchemy, was published a year after Herbert's death in 1633, and much later set to music as a hymn ('Teach me my God and King'). Although the meaning now seems fairly straightforward as a young boy I didn't understand what this verse was about and my school music teacher tried to explain it by using the simple image of glass in a window on which you could focus your gaze or with imagination look through the glass and see the wonders of the wider world beyond. It could also mean 'glass' as in 'looking-glass' or mirror, a plea to look through your own self to see the larger perspective or, in religious terms, the Kingdom of Heaven.

Looking up I found I had no sense of perspective, the stars seemed to all be the same distance from me making me feel like the focus of the things I was seeing. This is not to describe a mystical experience, rather a confusing visual sensation.

In an essay on Vladimir Tatlin's work Margit Rowell talks about a similar effect:

'In conventional Western art perspective may be designed in terms of a pyramid of space. The tip of the pyramid is at the furthest point of depth, behind the object and therefore penetrates the wall. In the icon the tip is in front of the object, in the viewer's eye, and the base of the pyramid is the wall's surface. Thus the icon's inverse perspective projected the object and its meaning into the viewers actual space, the space of existential experience.'

Confronted with the bewildering mass of stars above my head I seemed to be experiencing something like this 'icon perspective' when, turning slightly, I noticed for the first time that a whole section of the sky was black and empty.

I woke early next morning, the air was freezing and the flow of the river noisier than ever. The tent was in deep shadow because just the other side of the rushing water, less than 50m away, the sheer wall of the mountain, invisible in the darkness of the previous night, rose vertically blocking out the sun, blocking out half the sky.

After breakfast we started the five-hour ascent to the top from where I could photograph four of the seven lakes stretching off into the far distance, different blues against the dusty brown of the mountains. I was an observer again, back behind the glass.

Here are a couple of photos from that trip into the mountains. Over the page the view from the top that day showing two of the lakes in the valley and, below, me cooling my feet in the shallows after we got back to camp.

In the Sainsbury collection the other day I had a moment where I felt quite low. I'm very familiar with the work on show there now and perhaps for that reason I was looking for something different, something I hadn't noticed before. It's difficult with a fixed collection for works to take you by surprise and it seemed that at that moment some of the life had gone out of certain of the pieces. For instance an Epstein head of a sleeping baby and a soapstone head from Sierra Leone, both quite near each other in the displays, took on the appearance of severed heads with their cleanly cut necks and closed eyes. A visual impression I remember you talking about in the past. Of course the captions nearby didn't mention anything about death or severed heads and I felt disappointed with myself for seeing them in that way.

Not far away I found a beautiful, finely carved torso from Cambodia. It is not very big, only 43cm high, and probably if you could put both hands round her waist you'd be able to touch your thumb and finger tips together. No head but full of life – she cheered me up.

With love from us all
John

from John Berger August 2012

12/8/12

Dear John,

I'm enchanted by the story of Alice playing her flute and the deer coming to listen. (Etymologically the word enchanted is surely connected to the notion of being taken in by a song or carried away by a song.) So she plays like Orpheus and the animals leave their forest. Have you got a picture of her playing her flute?

If I'm not mistaken (could be) Tilda Swinton told me that she's about to play in a film which tells the story of the doomed expedition with the Red Tent. And she was wondering what it would be like to shoot — and play — in arctic temperatures.

The quotations from your friend

Gael is so appropriate (adequate) to
Eugenia's Balcell's project. Dali asked
me to write something too - and I sent
her a page I had written about a
mosaic in Ravenna. Tell me more
about Gael. I love the print - which
is not an "illustration". It's a
self-contained drama. About what happens
to a certain red when it encounters
a certain black. And this drama
runs parallel to the lines he quotes
from his poem. The whole poem is
where? The print and the lines are
both about fragility and persistence,
are'nt they? About the nature of
endurance.

During ~~the World~~ World War II,
when there was a "black-out" in London,
and when, during an air-raid, the
street lamps were turned off or
radically diminished, the Londoners
who were still in London, looked up
at the sky and were "enchanted" by
the exceptional brightness of the stars.

3.

What a journey, yours in 1992, to Tashkent and Tajikistan! And what a confirmation of Gael's lines is the story of Ulugh Beg's observatory! And you talk about distances and sounds ~~noise~~, Niagras! And somehow to me this is significant, for the two somehow go together. The sound of the flute travelled quite a distance to bring the deer out of their forest.

George Herbert's poem is about seeing beyond, yes. Yet from the beyond something comes towards us. Something unpronounceable but relevant. We receive ~~something~~ like an echo of our will to go, to look, to imagine beyond. And this something although inaudible is musical. Or, to put it another way, its modalities are nearer to those of music than to those of anything else we know.

Your breathing photo of the two lakes is redolent of such an echo. Compare it to the Cambodian Torso. Both refer to a Here; both reply to a beyond. Without referring (Thank Heaven!) to any eschatological arguments.

4 .

Yesterday I was writing about something which happened last week. And suddenly now I want to put it in here. Inaudible music.

Eight o clock on a summer evening in a metro train heading for a Parisian suburb. There are no empty seats but the standing passengers are not crammed together. Four men in their mid-twenties are standing in a group near the sliding doors on the right-hand side of the coach, the doors which dont open when the train is running in this direction.

One of the group is black, two are white and the fourth is perhaps maghrebian. I'm standing quite a distance away from them. What first caught my attention was their very visible connivance and the intensity of their conversation and story-telling.

The four are casually but scrupulously dressed. What they look like, their appearances, would seem to matter to them even more than to most men of their age. Everything about them is alert, nothing is hang dog. The magrebian is wearing loose blue shorts and spotless nylus. The black has combed meshes, the colour of sandalwood, in his thick black hair. All four are virile and masculine.

(5) The train stops and a few passengers get out. I can move a little closer to the quartet.

Each intervenes frequently in the recital of each of the others. There are no monologues but equally nothing seems to be an interruption. Their fingers, very mobile, are often near their faces.

Suddenly it dawns on me that they are stone deaf. It was their fluency which prevented me from realising this before.

Another station. They find four seats together. I stood, close, behind them ⊙ ~~close now~~. They continue to behave as if they were alone. Yet the manner in which they decide to ignore the rest of us, is a form of tact and politeness, not of indifference.

I glance up and down the coach. It seems that I'm the only person who has noticed them. In the metro one seldom listens to what other passengers are saying And so if the language being used is ~~A SILENT ME~~, there is nothing remarkable to notice. Occasionally one of the four grunts with laughter.

Their story-telling, their commentary on events continues. I am now watching ~~watch~~ them as curiously as they are watching each other.

(6) They share a vocabulary of gestural signs to replace a vocabulary of pronounced words, and their vocabulary of theirs has its own syntax and grammar, mostly established by timing. Their gestural signals are made with their hands, faces and bodies, which take over the function of both tongue and ear, of one organ which articulates and the other which receives. In any sustained dialogue anywhere both are equally important. Yet in the entire coach, probably in the entire train, there is no dialogue taking place, comparable to theirs.

Each physical feature with which the quartet gestures in order to converse — eye, upper lip, lower lip, teeth, chin, brow, thumb, finger, wrist shoulder — each feature has for them the range of a musical instrument or of a voice, with all its specific notes, chords, trills and degrees of insistance and hesitancy. Watching them one's eyes is like listening with one's ears to a jam session.

Yet in my ears there is only the sound of the train which is slowing down for the next stop. Several passengers are getting to their feet. I could sit but I prefer to stay where I am. The quartet are of course aware of my presence. One of them gives me a smile, not of welcome, but of acquiescence.

Intercepting their myriad exchanges, to which I can give no name, following their responses back and forth whilst remaining ignorant about what they refer to, swinging to their rhythm, carried forward by their expectancy, I have the sensation of being surrounded by a song, a song born of their solitude, a song in a foreign language. A song without sound.

With love to you all and thank you, Alice! John.

Dear John

I'm enchanted by the story of Alice playing her flute and the deer coming to listen. (Etymologically the word *enchanted* is surely connected to the notion of being taken in by a song or carried away by a song). So she plays like Orpheus and the animals leave their forest. Have you got a picture of her playing her flute? If I'm not mistaken (could be) Tilda Swinton told me that she's about to play in a film which tells the story of the doomed expedition with the Red Tent. And she was wondering what it would be like to shoot – and play – in arctic temperatures.

The question from your friend Gael is so appropriate (adequate) to Eugenia Balcell's project. Lali asked me to write something too – and I sent her a page I'd written about a mosaic in Ravenna. Tell me more about Gael. I love the print which is not an 'illustration'. It's a self-contained drama. About what happens to a certain red when it encounters a certain black. And this drama runs parallel to the lines he quotes from his poem. The whole poem is where? The print and the lines are both about fragility and persistence, aren't they? About the nature of endurance.

During World War II, when there was a 'black-out' in London, and when, during an air-raid, the street lamps were turned off or radically diminished, the Londoners who were still in London looked up at the sky and were 'enchanted' by the exceptional brightness of the stars.

What a journey, yours in 1992, to Tashkent and Tajikistan! And what a confirmation of Gael's lines in the story of Ulugh Beg's observatory! And you talk about distances and about sounds, Niagara's! And somehow to me this is significant, for the two somehow go together. The sound of the flute travelled quite a distance to bring the deer out of their forest.

George Herbert's poem is about seeing beyond, yes. Yet from the beyond something comes towards us. Something unpronounceable but relevant. We receive something like an echo of our will to go, to look, to imagine beyond. And this something although inaudible is musical. Or, to put it another way, its modalities are nearer to those of music than to those of anything else we know.

Your breathing photo of the two lakes is redolent of such an echo. Compare it to the Cambodian *Torso*. Both refer to a there; both reply to a beyond. Without referring (Thank Heaven!) to any eschatological arguments.

Yesterday I was writing about something that happened last week. And suddenly now I want to put it in here. Inaudible music.

Eight o'clock on a summer evening in a metro train heading for a Parisian suburb. There are no empty seats but the standing passengers are not crammed together. Four men in their mid-twenties are standing in a group near the sliding doors on the right-hand side of the coach. The doors which don't open when the train is running in this direction.

One of the group is black, two are white and the fourth is perhaps Maghribian. I'm standing quite a distance away from them. What first caught my attention was their very visible connivance and the intensity of their conversation and story-telling.

The four are casually but scrupulously dressed. What they look like, their appearances, would seem to matter to them even more than to most men of their age. Everything about them is alert, nothing is hangdog. The Maghribian is wearing loose blue shorts and spotless Nikes. The black has combed meshes, the colour of sandalwood, in his thick black hair. All four are virile and masculine.

The train stops and a few passengers get out. I can move a little closer to the quartet.
Each intervenes frequently in the recital of each of the others. There are no monologues but equally nothing seems to be an interruption. Their fingers, very mobile, are often near their faces. Suddenly it dawns on me that they are stone deaf. It was their fluency which prevented me from realising this before.

Another station. They find four seats together. I stand close behind them. They continue to behave as if they were alone. Yet the manner in which they decide to ignore the rest of us, is a form of tact and politeness, not of indifference.

I glance up and down the coach. It seems as though I'm the only person who has noticed them. In the metro one seldom listens to what other passengers are saying. And so if the language being used is a silent one there is nothing remarkable to notice. Occasionally one of the four grunts with laughter.
Their story-telling, their commentary on events continues. I am now watching them as curiously as they are watching each other.

They share a vocabulary of gestural signs to replace a vocabulary of pronounced words, and this vocabulary of theirs has its own syntax and grammar, mostly established by timing. Their gestural signals are made with their hands, faces and bodies which take over the function of both tongue and ear, of one organ that articulates and the other that receives. In any sustained dialogue anywhere both are equally important. Yet in the entire coach, probably in the entire train, there is no dialogue taking place comparable to theirs.

Each physical feature with which the quartet gestures in order to converse – eye, upper lip, lower lip, teeth, chin, brow, thumb, finger, wrist, shoulder – each feature has for them the range of a musical instrument or of a voice, with all its specific notes, chords, trills and degrees of insistence and hesitancy. Watching them with one's eyes is like listening with one's ears to a jam session.

Yet in my ears there is only the sound of the train which is slowing down for the next stop. Several passengers are getting to their feet. I could sit but prefer to stay where I am. The quartet are of course aware of my presence. One of them gives me a smile, not of welcome, but of acquiescence.

Intercepting their myriad exchanges, to which I can give no name, following their responses back and forth whilst remaining ignorant about what they refer to, swinging to the rhythm, carried forward by their expectancy, I have the sensation of being surrounded by a song, a song born of their solitude, a song in a foreign language. A song without sound.

With love to you all and thank you, Alice!
John

from John Christie September 2012

At a Frontier

Dear John

As I read your letter about the encounter in the
train carriage it brought to my mind a strong image
of you standing at a frontier, a border between
sound and silence. You shadowing the group in the
noisy carriage, not as invisibly as you hoped as
one of the men eventually acknowledged you, sharing
a glance of recognition across the frontier – maybe
he assumed you were deaf as well and somehow in
the same boat? By catching your eye for a moment
he must have missed part of the ongoing story.

What you wrote made me think immediately of the
work of Juan Muñoz. The silence that pervades it,
the feeling of being invisible or unseen, with
always the possibility that his enigmatic figures,
against the odds, will turn and acknowledge you
(as the deaf man did) as you wander past them; men
sitting with their backs to you, people listening
in corners, figures with their ears glued to the
wall, assembled crowds of Chinese men laughing and
talking together. Do you remember the film 'Wings
of Desire' and the ease with which the angels
moved about undetected in our everyday world?

I imagine Juan to have had a very good sense of
humour. I remember reading a story somewhere (I've
tried to find it for accuracy's sake but couldn't
lay my hands on it) about his search for a dwarf
to be the model for a new series of works. At his
local bar he asked if the barman knew of anyone
and he gave Juan the phone number of one of his
regulars who happened to be a dwarf and suggested
giving him a call. When they eventually spoke on
the phone and arranged to meet at another bar the
dwarf asked him, 'How will I recognise you?'

This photo I took at Quincy, the small figures on

the shelf in the corner, they must be by Juan? You
worked together on various projects, including
'*Will It Be A Likeness*' - have you got a favourite
story about him?

You ask about Gael Turnbull's 'universe' poem that I quoted and I think that it was a thing in itself rather than part of a longer work. I've looked through his *Collected Poems* but couldn't spot it either as a fragment or a complete piece. At the time I asked him if he had a short text I could use on a card and this was one of the poems he sent me to choose from. That was one of the things I liked about him, I could ask for a piece of writing about almost any subject (although in this case I don't remember specifying anything in particular) and he would always come up with something interesting.

We made a few books together with Circle Press, sometimes from texts he already had to hand but often from suggestions I made to him during discussions we had between us. Here is a photo I took of Gael outside the Circle workshop in Notting Hill in 1992 catching him mid-conversation.

We first met, after exchanging a few letters, in the very early '80s at an event at Coracle, a gallery and publisher in Camberwell New Road. It was snowing on the day of the reading and when I phoned to see if it had been cancelled was told Gael was definitely on his way. The fact that he was braving the weather to come from Stratford-upon-Avon spurred me into making a journey through the snow from west London.

I recall at one point that evening he recited from memory, much to everyone's delight, a long Icelandic saga. He was a good performer with a gentle but commanding voice – perhaps this came from his training as a doctor – and an easy person to like. From that evening we became firm friends.

Gael was born in 1928 and his family moved from Scotland (his father was a minister) to Canada where he grew up. He graduated as a doctor at the University of Pennsylvania in the early '50s but moved back up to Canada in 1952 to avoid the draft for the Korean War and worked as a GP in towns and logging camps in north Ontario. During this time he made contact with another doctor/poet, William Carlos Williams, whose writing influenced him greatly, and also linked up with many of the younger writers like Robert Creeley, Gary Snyder and Cid Corman. He started his own publishing venture, Migrant Press, and when he finally moved back to England in 1964 he introduced many of these American poets for the first time to the British audience through Migrant, as well as bringing Scottish writers like Ian Hamilton Finlay and Edwin Morgan to the attention of the Americans.

He was still working as a doctor when we first met but retired in 1989 and moved with his wife Jill to Edinburgh. I'm sure he enjoyed the balancing act and stimulation of collaboration. As well as a steady stream of his own work in small-press poetry books he also made very immediate little booklets, duplicated or photocopied and stapled together. These 'Minimal Missives' as he called them would be sent to a few friends and were always a delight to receive. It was his way of quietly releasing his work out into the world.

In one way I quite envied his ability to produce these little pamphlets from typing paper or what-ever was to hand and not be overly concerned or side-tracked like me with the layout, printing and assembling of things. Here's a photocopy of a poem (the original from him a photocopy too) send just before Christmas '99 which gives a flavour of these 'missives'.

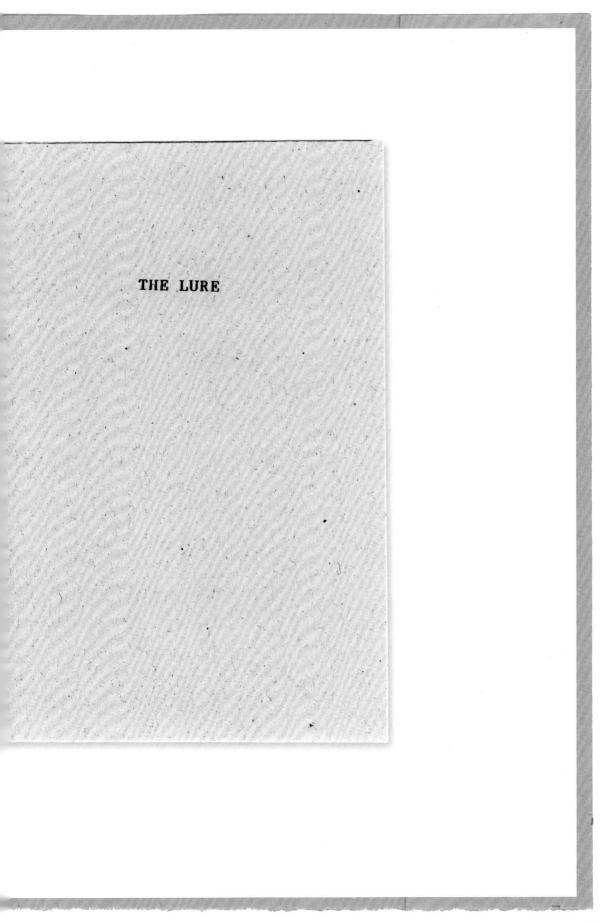

THE LURE

Gael was born in 1928 and his family moved from
Scotland (his father was a minister) to Canada
where he grew up. He graduated as a doctor at the
University of Pe
moved back up to
for the Korean W
logging camps in
he made contact
Carlos Williams,
greatly, and als
younger writers
and Cid Corman.
venture, Migrant
back to England
these American p
British audience
Scottish writers
Edwin Morgan to

He was still wor
but retired in 1
to Edinburgh. I'
act and stimulat
a steady stream
poetry books he
booklets, duplic
together. These
them would be se
a delight to rec
releasing his wo

In one way I qui
these little pam
ever was to hand
side-tracked lik
and assembling c
poem (the original from him a photocopy too) send
just before Christmas '99 which gives a flavour
of these 'missives'.

with very best for
that
whatever-it-is –

at whatever line –

Gael

The lure

Always the lure
of just one poem
more... as if the
reshuffled words
might yet disturb
whatever it is
we're persisting for?

One interest I didn't share with him was his love
of Morris dancing which he'd taken up for exercise
after a bout of polio contracted, oddly enough,
while working at a hospital back in England in
1955. I never really understood this attraction
until his wife Jill told me recently that aside
from the exercise element he loved the fact that
social status didn't come into the equation, as
long as you were part of the Morris team and could
dance nobody cared whether you were a doctor or a
dustman. He was quite passionate about it and when,
before retiring, he moved to his last medical
practice in Ulverston, Cumbria he was delighted to
tell me in a letter that he'd discovered a local
Morris group in the town and immediately signed up.

His work often contained fragments from found
texts which he described as 'texturalist'...
'in that they make a fresh pattern or texture out
of previously existing texts. Thus the final
result, if inevitably having something of my own,
is a tribute to the original and the voice of
someone else, and is a way of exploring
possibilities beyond my own unaided invention.'

He often stayed with us when in London and I
remember well his soft voice talking about books,
exhibitions and mutual friends over a leisurely
breakfast before he set off to St. Pancras for the
journey home, invariably stopping off at the
British Library to visit another friend on the way.

Every year at the Edinburgh Festival he would
perform in the street, reading his work to
passers-by or operating one of the kinetic poetry
machines he made. A little while before he died
from a sudden brain haemorrhage in 2004 he made a
rather beautiful poetry installation, printed
words that encircled a round goldfish pond in the

Kibble Botanical Gardens in Glasgow. A text that could only be read as a reflection.

I have four or five box files full of his letters and our finished and half-finished projects sitting in my studio. I'll give them to the National Library of Scotland, who have the rest of his papers, at some point, but for the time being I keep them with me. I know there are several potential books tucked away in those files of letters from him.

Going through the last file the other day when I was thinking about writing about him to you I found this short paragraph from one of his final letters, which gives an indication of his constant curiosity. I'd been telling him about a film I'd been making on the new ocean liner Queen Mary 2:

'Yes, the high seas. Why "high"? The waves? Or is this some resonance from staring at horizons without any feature which often have the feeling of being slightly higher than the level at which one sees them... There is also the way a ship appears coming over the horizon, as if coming up hill...'

His great friend, the poet Roy Fisher, wrote this of Gael and it sums up what I feel about him too:

'Of all my lost friends he is the least dead. The unique pace of his mind, sometimes troubled, always curious, seems still to be keeping us company somewhere just out of reach.'

Here's an adaptation he made after the French writer Jacques Charpentreau.
His friend and editor Hamish Whyte said of it:

'*Do You* is typically Turnbull: sparked by another work (he was a great homager), full of repetition, a sing-song quality, a wry humour, an enticing simplicity saying profound things.'

Do You

Do you see who dodges away,
disappearing into the blue?
That is life, on its way,
  dancing beyond you.

Do you feel a breath tease
your cheek, stir the grass, lift the dew?
That is time, like the breeze,
  having fun with you.

Do you hear singing, a choir
of echoing voices, promising anew?
Relax. That is only desire
  playing tricks with you.

Do you sense at your elbow
an old friend but can't guess who?
That is death, faithful shadow,
  laughing with you.

One morning recently I found a dead song thrush,
looking as though it was frozen in flight, skimming
the flag stones just outside my studio. At first I
though it might have been killed by our cat but
came to think, because of its untroubled appearance,
that it must have crashed into the windows,
confused by the reflection of the landscape and
sky, and died of a broken neck. Over the next few
days this same thing happened several times
although luckily on the other occasions the birds
just knocked themselves out, recovered after a
while, and flew off. I took a photo of the thrush
and then, because it seemed too beautiful to just
throw in the hedge, put it on a sheet of card and
placed it in my studio out of the sun so that I
could have a good look at it later.

When I went back next day there was a strong, sickly smell in the room and the bird's feathers were moving, crawling with maggots. That smell hung around for the next few days even though the windows were open and the dead bird and its live companions were now consigned to the ditch.

Being generally poor at identifying wild creatures, plants or trees, except the very common ones, I had to look up to confirm that it actually was a song thrush and then of course came upon a whole sea of references, mythologies and facts, concerning the bird, beginning with its scientific name, *Turdus philomelos*. The unfortunate sounding *Turdus* being the Latin for thrush and *philomelos* from the Greek mythological character *Philomela* who was changed into a songbird after her tongue was cut out. *Philomela* in turn coming from *philo* meaning *love* and *melos* meaning *song* and so on and so on. But forget that interesting language baggage and look again at the photo of the bird itself and you'll see such perfection, the reason, probably, that I was blind to the possibility of the flies spotting it first.

My ignorance of animals and plants I could blame on living in the city for most of my life, although when I was a kid and in the Boy Scouts I seem to remember being able to readily identify trees and plants and the tracks of animals and birds, but that was probably the result of having to take in the knowledge to pass a badge.

I've been reading Robert Macfarlane's *The Old Ways*, a meditation on walking and the ancient pathways and routes that cross the surface of the earth both on land and sea. Some of the journeys he makes follow in the footsteps of the poet Edward Thomas, in an effort to try to understand better Thomas and his work, others take him to visit places outside the UK including a trip to Palestine to walk with his friend Raja Shehadeh.

'Raja had been walking the hills and paths of the Ramallah region for more than forty years. When he began walking, before the Six-Day War of 1967, the appearance of the hills was largely unchanged from the time of the Roman occupation, and it was possible for him to move more or less unimpeded among them: to conduct what in Arabic is known as a *sarha*. In its original verb-form, *sarha* meant "to let the cattle out to pasture early in the morning, allowing them to wander and graze freely". It was subsequently humanised to suggest the action of a walker who went roaming without constraint or fixed plan. One might think the English equivalent to be a "stroll", an "amble" or a "ramble", but these words don't quite catch the implications of escape, delight and improvisation that are carried by *sarha*. "Wander" comes close, with its shadow-word of "wonder"... but best of all perhaps is "saunter", from the French *sans terre*, which is a contraction of *à la sainte terre*, meaning "to the sacred place"; i.e. "a walking pilgrimage". Saunter and *sarha* both have surface connotations of aimlessness, and smuggled connotations of the spiritual.'

I don't think that my own walks around the wood have either of these characteristics of aimlessness or spirituality but they certainly help me to concentrate and collect my thoughts together, which is another thread in *The Old Ways* concerning the pace of walking and its ability to stimulate ideas.

Robert Macfarlane also writes about the ancient sea-roads and this brought to mind first the BBC's late-night Shipping Forecast and then a poem by

Seamus Heaney which begins with names from that
hypnotic, clockwise list; a list that takes you on
a journey each time you hear it broadcast. Anyone
who listened to the radio when growing up would
know the order by heart in the same way that they
would know by repetition their eight and nine
times table. Names of places and regions far away
accompanied by their gale and fog warnings, places
unvisited and lost... Heligoland (long replaced in
the forecast by German Bight), Dogger (the ancient
submerged area, now called Doggerland by the
archaeologists and once part of the land-bridge
that connected Britain to Europe) and The Faroes,
some of the names that still stick in my mind. I
made a short TV film about this poem and its
corrected and worked-over manuscript and while
doing so listened to the recording of Seamus'
voice reading it many times.

Glanmore Sonnet VII

Dogger, Rockall, Malin, Irish Sea:
Green, swift upsurges, North Atlantic flux
Conjured by that strong gale-warning voice,
Collapse into a sibilant penumbra.
Midnight and closedown. Sirens of the tundra,
Of eel-road, seal-road, keel-road, whale-road, raise
Their wind-compounded keen behind the baize
And drive the trawlers to the lee of Wicklow.
L'Etoile, *Le Guillemot*, *La Belle Hélène*
Nursed their bright names this morning in the bay
That toiled like mortar. It was marvellous
And actual, I said out loud, 'A haven,'
The word deepening, clearing, like the sky
Elsewhere on Minches, Cromarty, The Faroes.

Thinking of Juan earlier and just now Seamus
Heaney and remembering different trips I've made
to Ireland too this small incident came back to me.

In 1994 I was in Dublin for some filming and on an
unexpected free afternoon while a casting session
was taking place I went out to Kilmainham to see
the Juan Muñoz exhibition at MOMA. By the time I'd
looked around the show which was spread about the
old hospital buildings and inner courtyard I
realised time was getting on and I needed to get
back to my hotel in the city centre. I decided on
a taxi as the quickest option but soon we were
stuck in heavy rush-hour traffic and the driver,
when he knew I was in a hurry, began to nip
through side streets in an effort to speed the
journey along. I've no idea whether this was
quicker or not but it had the effect of feeling it
was as we kept more or less constantly on the
move. All the while the driver chatted over his
shoulder, giving me a running commentary on the
places we were passing. At one point in a narrow
back street, close by St. Patrick's Cathedral, he
pointed to a door and said 'You see that door,
behind that door is the oldest public library in
Europe, a magnificent place, almost three hundred
years old. And', he emphasised 'it's here in
Dublin.' I was quite impressed by his obvious
pride in the library and asked what it was like
inside, 'I haven't a clue, I imagine it's just
full of old books'.

with love from us all
John

Dear John

As I read your letter about the encounter in the train carriage it brought to my mind a strong image of you standing at a frontier, a border between sound and silence. You shadowing the group in the noisy carriage, not as invisibly as you hoped as one of the men eventually acknowledged you, sharing a glance of recognition across the frontier – maybe he assumed you were deaf as well and somehow in the same boat? By catching your eye for a moment he must have missed part of the ongoing story.

What you wrote made me think immediately of the work of Juan Muñoz. The silence that pervades it, the feeling of being invisible or unseen, with always the possibility that his enigmatic figures, against the odds, will turn and acknowledge you (as the deaf man did) as you wander past them; men sitting with their backs to you, people listening in corners, figures with their ears glued to the wall, assembled crowds of Chinese men laughing and talking together. Do you remember the film '*Wings of Desire*' and the ease with which the angels moved about undetected in our everyday world?

I imagine Juan to have had a very good sense of humour. I remember reading a story somewhere (I've tried to find it for accuracy's sake but couldn't lay my hands on it) about his search for a dwarf to be the model for a new series of works. At his local bar he asked if the barman knew of anyone and he gave Juan the phone number of one of his regulars who happened to be a dwarf and suggested giving him a call. When they eventually spoke on the phone and arranged to meet at another bar the dwarf asked him, 'How will I recognise you?'

This photo I took at Quincy, the small figures on the shelf in the corner, they must be by Juan? You worked together on various projects, including '*Will It Be A Likeness*' – have you got a favourite story about him?

You ask about Gael Turnbull's 'universe' poem that I quoted and I think that it was a thing in itself rather than part of a longer work. I've looked through his *Collected Poems* but couldn't spot it either as a fragment or a complete piece. At the time I asked him if he had a short text I could use on a card and this was one of the poems he sent me to choose from. That was one of the things I liked about him, I could ask for a piece of writing about almost any subject (although in this case I don't remember specifying anything in particular) and he would always come up with something interesting.

We made a few books together with Circle Press, sometimes from texts he already had to hand but often from suggestions I made to him during discussions we had between us. Here is a photo I took of Gael outside the Circle workshop in Notting Hill in 1992 catching him mid-conversation.

We first met, after exchanging a few letters, in the very early '80s at an event at Coracle, a gallery and publishers in Camberwell New Road. It was snowing on the day of the reading and when I phoned to see if it had been cancelled was told Gael was definitely on his way. The fact that he was braving the weather to come from Stratford-upon-Avon spurred me into making a journey through the snow from west London.

I recall at one point that evening he recited from memory, much to everyone's delight, a long Icelandic saga. He was a good performer with a gentle but commanding voice – perhaps this came from his training as a doctor – and an easy person to like. From that evening we became firm friends.

Gael was born in 1928 and his family moved from Scotland (his father was a minister) to Canada where he grew up. He graduated as a doctor at the University of Pennsylvania in the early '50s but moved back up to Canada in 1952 to avoid the draft for the Korean War and worked as a GP in towns and logging camps in north Ontario. During this time he made contact with another doctor/poet, William Carlos Williams, whose writing influenced him greatly, and also linked up with many of the younger writers like Robert Creeley, Gary Snyder and Cid Corman. He started his own publishing venture, Migrant Press, and when he finally moved back to England in 1964 he introduced many of these American poets for the first time to the British audience through Migrant, as well as bringing Scottish writers like Ian Hamilton Finlay and Edwin Morgan to the attention of the Americans.

He was still working as a doctor when we first met but retired in 1989 and moved with his wife Jill to Edinburgh. I'm sure he enjoyed the balancing act and stimulation of collaboration. As well as a steady stream of his own work in small-press poetry books he also made very immediate little booklets, duplicated or photocopied and stapled together. These 'Minimal Missives' as he called them would be sent to a few friends and were always a delight to receive. It was his way of quietly releasing his work out into the world.

In one way I quite envied his ability to produce these little pamphlets from typing paper or whatever was to hand and not be overly concerned or side-tracked like me with the layout, printing and assembling of things. Here's a photocopy of a poem (the original from him a photocopy too) send just before Christmas '99 which gives a flavour of these 'missives'.

One interest I didn't share with him was his love of Morris dancing which he'd taken up for exercise after a bout of polio contracted, oddly enough, while working at a hospital back in England in 1955. I never really understood this attraction until his wife Jill told me recently that aside from the exercise element he loved the fact that social status didn't come into the equation, as long as you were part of the Morris team and could dance nobody cared whether you were a doctor or a dustman. He was quite passionate about it and when, before retiring, he moved to his last medical practice in Ulverston, Cumbria he was delighted to tell me in a letter that he'd discovered a local Morris group in the town and immediately signed up.

His work often contained fragments from found texts which he described as 'texturalist'... 'in that they make a fresh pattern or texture out of previously existing texts. Thus the final result, if inevitably having something of my own, is a tribute to the original and the voice of someone else, and is a way of exploring possibilities beyond my own unaided invention.'

He often stayed with us when in London and I remember well his soft voice talking about books, exhibitions and mutual friends over a leisurely breakfast before he set off to St. Pancras for the journey home, invariably stopping off at the British Library to visit another friend on the way.

Every year at the Edinburgh Festival he would perform in the street, reading his work to passers-by or operating one of the kinetic poetry machines he made. A little while before he died from a sudden brain haemorrhage in 2004 he made a rather beautiful poetry installation, printed words that encircled a round goldfish pond in the Kibble Botanical Gardens in Glasgow. A text that could only be read as a reflection.

I have four or five box files full of his letters and our finished and half-finished projects sitting in my studio. I'll give them to the National Library of Scotland, who have the rest of his papers, at some point, but for the time being I keep them with me. I know there are several potential books tucked away in those files of letters from him.

Going through the last file the other day when I was thinking about writing about him to you I found this short paragraph from one of his final letters, which gives an indication of his constant curiosity. I'd been telling him about a film I'd been making on the new ocean liner Queen Mary 2:

'Yes, the high seas. Why "high"? The waves? Or is this some resonance from staring at horizons without any feature which often have the feeling of being slightly higher than the level at which one sees them... There is also the way a ship appears coming over the horizon, as if coming up hill...'

His great friend, the poet Roy Fisher, wrote this of Gael and it sums up what I feel about him too:

'Of all my lost friends he is the least dead. The unique pace of his mind, sometimes troubled, always curious, seems still to be keeping us company somewhere just out of reach.'

Here's an adaptation he made after the French writer Jacques Charpentreau.
His friend and editor Hamish Whyte said of it:

'Do You is typically Turnbull: sparked by another work (he was a great homager), full of repetition, a sing-song quality, a wry humour, an enticing simplicity saying profound things.'

Do You

Do you see who dodges away,
disappearing into the blue?
That is life, on its way,
   dancing beyond you.

Do you feel a breath tease
your cheek, stir the grass, lift the dew?
That is time, like the breeze,
   having fun with you.

Do you hear singing, a choir
of echoing voices, promising anew?
Relax. That is only desire
   playing tricks with you.

Do you sense at your elbow
an old friend but can't guess who?
That is death, faithful shadow,
   laughing with you.

One morning recently I found a dead song thrush, looking as though it was frozen in flight, skimming the flag stones just outside my studio. At first I though it might have been killed by our cat but came to think, because of its untroubled appearance, that it must have crashed into the windows, confused by the reflection of the landscape and sky, and died of a broken neck. Over the next few days this same thing happened several times although luckily on the other occasions the birds just knocked themselves out, recovered after a while, and flew off. I took a photo of the thrush and then, because it seemed too beautiful to just throw in the hedge, put it on a sheet of card and placed it in my studio out of the sun so that I could have a good look at it later.

When I went back next day there was a strong, sickly smell in the room and the bird's feathers were moving, crawling with maggots. That smell hung around for the next few days even though the windows were open and the dead bird and its live companions were now consigned to the ditch.

Being generally poor at identifying wild creatures, plants or trees, except the very common ones, I had to look up to confirm that it actually was a song thrush and then of course came upon a whole sea of references, mythologies and facts, concerning the bird, beginning with its scientific name, Turdus philomelos. The unfortunate sounding Turdus being the Latin for thrush and from the Greek mythological character Philomela who was changed into a songbird after her tongue was cut out. Philomela in turn coming from philo meaning love and melos meaning song and so on and so on. But forget that interesting language baggage and look again at the photo of the bird itself and you'll see such perfection, the reason, probably, that I was blind to the possibility of the flies spotting it first.

My ignorance of animals and plants I could blame on living in the city for most of my life, although when I was a kid and in the Boy Scouts I seem to remember being able to readily identify trees and plants and the tracks of animals and birds, but that was probably the result of having to take in the knowledge to pass a badge.

I've been reading Robert Macfarlane's The Old Ways, a meditation on walking and the ancient pathways and routes that cross the surface of the earth both on land and sea. Some of the journeys he makes follow in the footsteps of the poet Edward Thomas, in an effort to try to understand better Thomas and his work, others take him to visit places outside the UK including a trip to Palestine to walk with his friend Raja Shehadeh.

'Raja had been walking the hills and paths of the Ramallah region for more than forty years. When he began walking, before the

Six-Day War of 1967, the appearance of the hills was largely unchanged from the time of the Roman occupation, and it was possible for him to move more or less unimpeded among them: to conduct what in Arabic is known as a *sarha*. In its original verb-form, *sarha* meant "to let the cattle out to pasture early in the morning, allowing them to wander and graze freely". It was subsequently humanised to suggest the action of a walker who went roaming without constraint or fixed plan. One might think the English equivalent to be a "stroll", an "amble" or a "ramble", but these words don't quite catch the implications of escape, delight and improvisation that are carried by *sarha*. "Wander" comes close, with its shadow-word of "wonder"... but best of all perhaps is "saunter", from the French *sans terre*, which is a contraction of *à la sainte terre*, meaning "to the sacred place"; i.e. "a walking pilgrimage". Saunter and *sarha* both have surface connotations of aimlessness, and smuggled connotations of the spiritual.'

I don't think that my own walks around the wood have either of these characteristics of aimlessness or spirituality but they certainly help me to concentrate and collect my thoughts together, which is another thread in *The Old Ways* concerning the pace of walking and its ability to stimulate ideas.

Robert Macfarlane also writes about the ancient sea-roads and this brought to mind first the BBC's late-night Shipping Forecast and then a poem by Seamus Heaney which begins with names from that hypnotic, clockwise list; a list that takes you on a journey each time you hear it broadcast. Anyone who listened to the radio when growing up would know the order by heart in the same way that they would know by repetition their eight and nine times table. Names of places and regions far away accompanied by their gale and fog warnings, places unvisited and lost... Heligoland (long replaced in the forecast by German Bight), Dogger (the ancient submerged area, now called Doggerland by the archaeologists and once part of the land-bridge that connected Britain to Europe) and The Faroes, some of the names that still stick in my mind. I made a short TV film about this poem and its corrected and worked-over manuscript and while doing so listened to the recording of Seamus' voice reading it many times.

Glanmore Sonnet VII

Dogger, Rockall, Malin, Irish Sea:
Green, swift upsurges, North Atlantic flux
Conjured by that strong gale-warning voice,
Collapse into a sibilant penumbra.
Midnight and closedown. Sirens of the tundra,
Of eel-road, seal-road, keel-road, whale-road, raise
Their wind-compounded keen behind the baize
And drive the trawlers to the lee of Wicklow.
L'Etoile, Le Guillemot, La Belle Hélène
Nursed their bright names this morning in the bay
That toiled like mortar. It was marvellous
And actual, I said out loud, 'A haven,'
The word deepening, clearing, like the sky
Elsewhere on Minches, Cromarty, The Faroes.

Thinking of Juan earlier and just now Seamus Heaney and remembering different trips I've made to Ireland too this small

incident came back to me.

In 1994 I was in Dublin for some filming and on an unexpected free afternoon while a casting session was taking place I went out to Kilmainham to see the Juan Muñoz exhibition at MOMA. By the time I'd looked around the show which was spread about the old hospital buildings and inner courtyard I realised time was getting on and I needed to get back to my hotel in the city centre. I decided on a taxi as the quickest option but soon we were stuck in heavy rush-hour traffic and the driver, when he knew I was in a hurry, began to nip through side streets in an effort to speed the journey along. I've no idea whether this was quicker or not but it had the effect of feeling it was as we kept more or less constantly on the move. All the while the driver chatted over his shoulder, giving me a running commentary on the places we were passing. At one point in a narrow back street, close by St. Patrick's Cathedral, he pointed to a door and said, 'You see that door, behind that door is the oldest public library in Europe, a magnificent place, almost three hundred years old. And', he emphasised 'it's here in Dublin.' I was quite impressed by his obvious pride in the library and asked what it was like inside, 'I haven't a clue, I imagine it's just full of old books'..

With love from us all
John

PS. Perhaps Tilda's Red Tent is the same story of the doomed *Italia* expedition. I've seen the Russian/Italian co-production made in 1969 starring amongst others Sean Connery, who played Amundsen, with the captain of the airship played by Peter Finch. In the film the crash and the survival on the ice were quite well done, considering they didn't use computer graphics, but most of my information came from reading. The twist in the story comes from the fact that, once the crash site was located and a light aircraft managed to land, the captain was persuaded by the journalist/pilot that the best course of action was for him to return in the plane to organise the rescue of the rest of his men. Unfortunately once back to safety he was accused of abandoning his crew and stripped of his command.

Birthday card for John Berger November 2012

Genevieve bought these two gourds in the market recently and they struck me as being quite Muñoz-like — either they are in conversation or looking at something together. They are to wish you a very happy birthday and to send you all our love.

John x

from John Berger November 2012

8/11/12

Dear John,

    I love the two gourds and thank you for their picture. You are right — they make me think of some of Juan's mysterious figures. And then you ask me about Juan himself.

    Maybe the first thing to tell about him is that he was a true and inveterate draughtsman. He knew how things fitted together and what held them together. Alongside his draughtsmanship his other considerable gift was that of a mechanic. He preferred to make something work rather than explain how it worked. Or to put this another way: I'd say Juan had the skills and the spirit of a great juggler.

    And this immediately raises the question: What did he juggle with? Figures, furniture, fittings — he loved displacing or misplacing things. A glance at his work makes this clear. Meet me in Istanbul, he would propose to me, and then we'll do something like .... Or : What about the Panama Canal, and from there with the two oceans we might .... Displacement and improvisation.

He was a juggler and, in imagination,
a globe-trotter, yet I believe that the
dimension which really challenged and fascinated
him was time. He wanted to stop the
moment. He wanted to bring us up short.
So that with him we could walk round the
instant and see it from all sides.

Juan has something in common with
your friend Gael Turnbull, the poet.

A story about him? Well, you see
the little rocking figures which you took a
picture of in the room upstairs. One time
when he came here and we were plotting
some intervention together, he brought them
with him. Yves was about eighteen at
the time, attending the art-school in
Geneva but mostly working by himself
at home. Juan as soon as he saw
Yves' first works encouraged him.
He took the rocking figures out of
his rucksack and gave them to Yves.
"They're for you", he said, "they are
unfinished and you have to finish them
In any way you like. If you want to
you can dress them. But finish them.
place them. The time to make a

masterpiece is now! You're ready!
Now! Not in five year's time."

He died suddenly, now ten years
ago. But as Roy Fisher said about Gael
"Of all my lost friends, he is the least
dead." He's improvising just behind or
just to one side of the present moment.

Gael's portrait which you sent in
your last letter makes him look like
a thought-reader. An oracle without
temple or tie. And the blue of the
background suits his expression so well.
Minimal Missives from the blue ...

Juan was often late for his
rendezvous. Twenty minutes, perhaps
half an hour. Not because he was
absent-minded. Least of all because
he was inconsiderate. But simply
because the last fix of an invention
took a little longer to fix than he had
calculated. And he was a scrupulous
mechanic.

Your photo of the song-thrush looks
like a painting, does'nt it? Maybe
because its feathers are like
brush-strokes? Philomela, who had her
tongue cut out so she could'nt tell
her sister that the King of Thrace had
raped her, also gave her name to the

nightingale and the swallow! Which
suggests that the myth-tellers were sometimes
as confused about species as us —
when we stopped being scouts! Yes,
I remember learning too about animal
tracks and signs — and having to choose
for oneself an animal or bird totem.
I chose Peewit or Lapwing which is a
bird of marshes and estuaries — and whose
call is Peeee — wit!

The Shipping forecast was like
a roll-call, no? Dogger! Present.
German Bight! Present. The Faroes!
Present. Every evening and morning.
And the distances were there inside
what was still called the wireless!
Of course for years I wanted when I
grew up to be a sailor. We were
attendant. Later, I wanted to
be a vet. What the two may
have in common — is the notion of
being (working) on a periphery,
rather than at a centre.

Yes, I met Raja Shehadeh
a couple of times in Palestine.
And what you say about the sarha
is so true. A way of keeping

unwritten appointments.

According to my dictionary
High Seas refers to the sea outside
Territorial waters.

And so again we return to
peripheries. Where most unwritten
appointments take place.

There's a song about a circle
falling in love with a line ....

Meanwhile my love to
you at Genevieve

John

Dear John

I love the two gourds and thank you for their picture. You are right – they make one think of some of Juan's mysterious figures. And then you ask me about Juan himself.

Maybe the first thing to tell about him is that he was a true and inveterate draughtsman. He knew how things fitted together and what held them together. Alongside his draughtsmanship his other considerable gift was that of a mechanic. He preferred to make something work rather than explain how it worked. Or to put this another way: I'd say Juan had the skills and the spirit of a great juggler.

And this immediately raises the question: what did he juggle with? Figures, furniture, fittings – he loved displacing or misplacing things. A glance at his work makes this clear. *Meet me in Istanbul,* he would propose to me, *and then we'll do something like...* Or: *what about the Panama Canal, and from there with the two oceans we might...* Displacement and improvisation.

He was a juggler and, in my imagination, a globe-trotter, yet I believe that the dimension which really challenged and fascinated him was time. He wanted to bring us up short. So that with him we could walk round the instant and see it from all sides.

Juan had something in common with your friend Gael Turnbull, the poet.

A story about him? Well you see the little rocking figures you took a picture of in the room upstairs. One time when he came here and we were plotting some intervention together, he brought these with him. Yves was about eighteen at the time, attending the art-school in Geneva but mostly working by himself at home. Juan as soon as he saw Yves' first works encouraged him. He took the rocking figures out of his rucksack and gave them to Yves. 'They're for you,' he said, 'they are unfinished and you have to finish them. In any way you like. If you want to, you can dress them. But finish them, place them. The time to make a masterpiece is now! You're ready! Now! Not in five year's time'.

He died suddenly, over ten years ago. But as Roy Fisher said about Gael 'Of all my lost friends, he is the least dead.' He's improvising just behind or just to one side of the present moment.

Gael's portrait which you sent in your last letter makes him look like a thought-reader. An oracle without temple or tie. And the blue of the background suits his expression so well. Minimal Missives from the blue..

Juan was often late for his rendezvous. Twenty minutes, perhaps half and hour. Not because he was absent-minded. Least of all because he was inconsiderate. But simply because the last fix of an invention took a little longer to fix than he had calculated. And he was a scrupulous mechanic.

Your photo of the song thrush looks like a painting, doesn't it? Maybe because its feathers are like brush-strokes? Philomela, who had her tongue cut out so she couldn't tell her sister that the King of Thrace had raped her, also gave her name to the nightingale and the swallow! Which suggests that the myth-tellers were sometimes as confused about species as us – when we stopped being scouts! Yes, I remember learning about animal tracks and signs – and having to choose for oneself an animal or bird totem. I chose Peewit or Lapwing which is a bird of marsh and estuaries – and whose call is Peee-wit!

The shipping forecast was like a roll-call, no? Dogger! Present. German Bight! Present. The Faroes! Present. Every evening and morning. And the distances were there inside what was still called the wireless! Of course for years I wanted when I grew up to be a sailor. We were attendant. Later, I wanted to be a vet. What the two may have in common is the notion of being (working) on the periphery, rather than at the centre.

Yes, I met Raja Shehadeh a couple of times in Palestine. And what you say about the *sarha* is so true. A way of keeping unwritten appointments.

According to my dictionary 'High Seas' refers to the sea outside territorial waters.

And so again we return to peripheries. Where most unwritten appointments take place.

There's a song about a circle falling in love with a line....

Meanwhile my love to you and Genevieve

John

from John Christie February 2013

Not Nature

Yes, I am lying in the ground, but my lips are moving, and what I say every schoolboy will learn

Osip Mandelstam – 'Red Square' Voronezh Notebooks

Art is above all not nature

Pierre Bonnard

Dear John

So you gave yourself the name lapwing, a bird of
the margins and, according to the RSPB, a declining
species in this country. I was a fox, or rather a
member of the fox patrol because I don't remember
choosing an individual creature for myself. The
fox is not in decline but not particularly welcome
in the countryside around here.

Every year a pair of pied wagtails appear at the
barn, spending a good proportion of their days in
full view, pacing backwards and forwards at
opposite ends of the ridge of the main roof. It
always brightens my day when I see them with
their constantly wagging tails and characteristic
jerky walk because they have been visiting here
since I first began work on the conversion of the
building and it's like seeing old friends when
they turn up. Remembering them, perhaps my
animal/bird totem should be a wagtail but ideally
I think I would choose an owl or a hare.

Juan and time. Your thought made me go back to
the catalogues to look again at photos of his
work and I realised that they, his sculptures and
groups of figures, have the feel of stills from a
film by which I mean they look as though they are
a slice of time, taken from a story or a puzzle.
Which is what I think you mean by 'with him we
could walk round the instant and see it from all
sides'. Except he often hides a side of the work,
against a wall or in a corner forcing the viewer
to see it from only the angle that he chooses.
And when you can walk around and through the
work, as in *Many Times*, the collection of smiling
Chinamen who look as though they've just emerged
from a conference to stretch their legs (until
you notice that they are frozen to the spot because

they don't have any feet), then you find that what you are witnessing throws up questions. It gives me sometimes the feeling of being locked out, witnessing but not being able to contribute.

Juan himself said, 'You're watching what's taking place, but you cannot answer back... You cannot collaborate in it...'

I wonder why he wanted that non-collaboration?

Many Times 1999

I emailed Gavin Bryars about Juan and he sent me
some photos plus this memory of him:

'One thing (that you might enjoy) is how much he
enjoyed performing *A Man in a Room, Gambling*
live. He was completely bemused by the experience
of being applauded for the work that he'd done
(it doesn't really happen that way in exhibitions
or private views). In fact the first time he ever
took a bow was before he started to perform live.
It was when I met John for the first time. We
performed *A Man in a Room, Gambling* and some
other works in the space of Juan's installation
at the Palacio Velásquez in Madrid. He and John
sat together in the front row of the audience and
I called him forward to take a bow at the end of
the performance. I was touched by how incoherent,
embarrassed and unformed his bow was, but he really
enjoyed the sight and feeling of public acclaim.
When we eventually did do the piece live he was
incredibly professional and went over and over
every detail both with the band and alone.'

Gavin also reminded me that *A Man in a Room, Gambling* had the link with '...that list of the maritime regions read out in sequence (which) forms a kind of litany' – the BBC Shipping Forecast – in that each five-minute segment of the piece was planned to be broadcast immediately before that evening's Shipping Forecast. He went on to say:

'Radio is a beautiful medium for many reasons. It stimulates the visual imagination; the listener can move between casual and attentive modes of listening; it moves inexorably through time, as well as being used as a way of measuring clock time (timing an egg to the duration of a news bulletin). It can also function as ambience, and indeed for a great deal of the time this is the preferred mode of attention for the 'listeners' of radio. On the other hand everyday life can equally serve as an unfocused (ambient) activity while the radio itself is playing – the preparation of a meal during a radio play for example.'

With time running out I made a trip to the south
coast to see the last week of an exhibition at
the De La Warr Pavilion in Bexhill-on-Sea. The
Pavilion, a Modernist icon right on the sea-front,
is in itself worth the journey. It was named
after the 9th Earl De La Warr, an interesting man
who instigated the project and was mayor of the
town in 1934 when the building was completed (he
was also the first hereditary peer to join the
Labour Party). Emigré architects Erich Mendelson
and Serge Chermayeff designed the building which
was listed Grade One in 2005 after years of neglect
and refurbished to its present impressive state.
It looks at its best on a clear sunny day but I
took this photo of it in the overcast mid-January
light to give you at least an idea of the place.

Dancing couples

de la warr
pavilion

Ian Brentnell

**KEEP THINGS
AS THEY ARE**

October 2012 – January 2013

The exhibition I was there to see was *Keep Things As They Are,* a retrospective of the work of artist, writer and film-maker Ian Breakwell. I worked with Ian on and off over the years, from the early 1980s up until 2002 three years before he died. One of his on-going projects was his *Continuous Diary*, which took many forms, being made up of paintings, photographs and texts in books and magazines. There was also a series of films of these diary entries, poignant funny/sad observations from everyday life, commissioned by Channel Four shortly after it started broadcasting in 1982. I filmed lots of these episodes with Ian as writer/presenter and our mutual friend, Anna Ridley, producing (you remember Anna produced *Another Way of Telling* for us too). The 'Diary' films were shown generally as the last programme of the day's television, after the religious Epilogue and before close-down. It's hard to imagine now a time when television felt the need for a religious homily to go with your bedtime cocoa and then actually shut down for the night. As the last broadcast programme Ian's films could be of any length and were usually around the 4-5 minutes mark with the longest one, if I remember correctly, running at 12 minutes, a film very critical of the Falklands War, and handed in to C4 by Anna at the last minute before transmission to avoid any censorship of the contents.

The main point of my journey to Ian's exhibition though was to watch *The Other Side*, a rarely-seen video installation which I shot for him at the De La Warr in 2002. It is a very moving 13 minute piece that transcends its component parts. Filmed from the top landing of the elegant staircase looking out towards the sea, the camera tracks slowly from side to side, parallel to the action, focussing on a group of elderly couples dancing

Couples on the balcony outside the window

Camera movement

around the outside of the topmost semi-circular balcony of the Pavilion to the sound of the sea and Schubert's Nocturne in E flat Major. Behind them is the backdrop of the late afternoon sky, beach and sea. The wind catches the dancers' hair and clothes as they waltz in slow-motion, seagulls cross the frame, people walk along the seafront in the distance and you glimpse the red 'no bathing' flag fluttering every now and then. Between the dancers and the camera the vertical stairwell light crosses frame continuously as the camera tracks slowly left and right and the lens follows the couples, sometimes in a wide shot with the chrome hand-rail of the stairs in foreground, sometimes in close-up as they dance and turn in each other's arms. After 13 minutes the screen fades to black and there is the sound of glass shattering (an audio reference to vandalism in this rather rundown seaside town) followed by the loud cry of seagulls startled by the noise. The elegiac mood of the piece is broken sharply. Then, after a short pause the screen fades up once more to the original tracking shot and the whole sequence begins again.

The installation, and this is why it is not seen often, uses a large double-sided screen (16ft x 9ft) which runs diagonally across a darkened space with access all round for the audience. The images are projected on both sides of the screen and differ from each other in that the dancers feature mainly on one side while the other side shows predominately the same tracking shot but empty, the dancers absent. The Schubert Nocturne fills the dark space. I watched the installation four times through, sometimes lost in the piece itself but also occasionally thinking about the making of it, the component parts that Ian put together with the help of the editor in such a magical way. The dancers were all local people who came to the tea dances every week. During the filming they waltzed on the chilly balcony, not to Schubert but to a rather cheesy CD of popular waltzes played on a theatre organ. My work on the camera was fairly straightforward although I recall struggling a little to maintain the visual continuity as later in the afternoon the winter sun began to set and the light levels changed, silhouetting the dancers against the horizon.

It was during his residency in 2000/01 at the De La Warr that Ian began to formulate the piece. He describes in an interview watching the dancing on the Pavilion terrace... 'elderly people would get up out of their deck-chairs with great difficulty and the music propels them along and they begin to glide. There is something incredibly moving and dignified about these elderly people who suddenly become graceful. And if it is two women dancing together there is a sadness to it as well because they'll probably both be widows. I began to think of a kind of dance in the fading light from sunset through to darkness.'

Ian was also obsessed with characters who live on the margins of society through either choice or bad luck. He felt that we were all only one or two chance turns of fate away from that margin. It was the subject of several of the films I shot for him. I never found it very easy filming people who were down on their luck and homeless because to catch the reality of a situation that can easily be seen by a quick glance of the eye is difficult when that glance has to be translated into the direct stare of the camera lens. Just the small courtesy of asking permission often risked the moment slipping away.

I've been rather preoccupied at the moment
preparing for an exhibition in April of new pastel
works on paper. They are non-figurative images of
overlapping planes of colour with elements of
geometry too but not in the sense of mathematical
geometry. Some were based initially on the visual
devices used in 'Dazzle' camouflage to disguise
shapes but as I'm not trying to hide anything in
that practical sense they are used now by me to
play off those beautiful, strong, dry colours
that only pastel produces. It's quite a laborious
process, which I won't go into here, because the
coloured powder of the pastels is hard to control
in this hard-edge way that I'm using it and the
works often technically fail and I have to start
again from scratch.

I am surrounded here by Nature with a capital 'N'
but have chosen in these works from the last
twelve months to turn my back on the world outside

the studio (my worktable physically faces away from the view), by occupying myself with questions of colour and shape. *Not Nature* was going to be my title for the exhibition but it was thought to be too negative, although I didn't mean it in a negative way only as a helpful definition of what the pictures were not about. I have been asking myself why I chose to take this direction away from the examples of Nature? Perhaps, besides being fascinated with the non-figurative work I'm doing at the moment, it's because I'm surrounded by something that I feel I cannot improve upon or represent in any way satisfactory to myself? Last year I stood listening to a bird singing in the hedge. It was a riveting, virtuoso performance that went on for quite a time, a complex, brilliantly inventive song that, had I been a composer, could have had the effect of making me feel hopelessly ill-equipped. Last weekend at one of the events celebrating Benjamin Britten's centenary I listened to a sound recording of birds singing in his garden and I heard the song again – it was a nightingale.

In this quote Olivier Messiaen (who knew a thing or two about birdsong and whose music I love) brings together Nature and some of the things I've been trying to talk about:

'.. music is a part of time, a fraction of time, as is our own life, and that Nature, ever beautiful, ever great, ever new, Nature, an inextinguishable treasure-house of sounds and colours, forms and rhythms, the unequalled model for total developments and perpetual variation, that Nature is the supreme resource.'

I look forward to hearing from you
with love from us all
John.

223

'Yes, I am lying in the ground, but my lips are moving, and what I say every schoolboy will learn'
Osip Mandelstam – *Voronezh Notebooks*

'Art is above all not nature'
Pierre Bonnard

Dear John
So you gave yourself the name lapwing, a bird of the margins and, according to the RSPB, a declining species in this country. I was a fox, or rather a member of the fox patrol because I don't remember choosing an individual creature for myself. The fox is not in decline but not particularly welcome in the countryside around here.

Every year a pair of pied wagtails appear at the barn, spending a good proportion of their days in full view, pacing backwards and forwards at opposite ends of the ridge of the main roof. It always brightens my day when I see them with their constantly wagging tails and characteristic jerky walk because they have been visiting here since I first began work on the conversion of the building and it's like seeing old friends when they turn up. Remembering them, perhaps my animal/bird totem should be a wagtail but ideally I think I would choose an owl or a hare.

Juan and time. Your thought made me go back to the catalogues to look again at photos of his work and I realised that they, his sculptures and groups of figures, have the feel of stills from a film by which I mean they look as though they are a slice of time, taken from a story or a puzzle. Which is what I think you mean by 'with him we could walk round the instant and see it from all sides'. Except he often hides a side of the work, against a wall or in a corner forcing the viewer to see it from only the angle that he chooses. And when you can walk around and through the work, as in *Many Times* , the collection of smiling Chinamen who look as though they've just emerged from a conference to stretch their legs (until you notice that they are frozen to the spot because they don't have any feet), then you find that what you are witnessing throws up questions. It gives me sometimes the feeling of being locked out, witnessing but not being able to contribute.

Juan himself said, 'You're watching what's taking place, but you cannot answer back... You cannot collaborate in it...'

I wonder why he wanted that non-collaboration?

I emailed Gavin Bryars about Juan and he sent me some photos plus this memory of him:
'One thing (that you might enjoy) is how much he enjoyed performing *A Man in a Room, Gambling* live. He was completely bemused by the experience of being applauded for the work that he'd done (it doesn't really happen that way in exhibitions or private views). In fact the first time he ever took a bow was before he started to perform live. It was when I met John for the first time. We performed *A Man in a Room, Gambling* and some other works in the space of Juan's installation at the Palacio Velásquez in Madrid. He and John sat together in the front row of the audience and I called him forward to take a bow at the end of the performance. I was touched by how incoherent, embarrassed and unformed his bow was, but he really enjoyed the sight and feeling of public acclaim. When we eventually did do the piece live he

was incredibly professional and went over and over every detail both with the band and alone.'

Gavin also reminded me that *A Man in a Room, Gambling* had the link with '... that list of the maritime regions read out in sequence (which) forms a kind of litany' – the BBC Shipping Forecast – in that each five-minute segment of the piece was planned to be broadcast immediately before that evening's Shipping Forecast. He went on to say:

'Radio is a beautiful medium for many reasons. It stimulates the visual imagination; the listener can move between casual and attentive modes of listening; it moves inexorably through time, as well as being used as a way of measuring clock time (timing an egg to the duration of a news bulletin). It can also function as ambience, and indeed for a great deal of the time this is the preferred mode of attention for the 'listeners' of radio. On the other hand everyday life can equally serve as an unfocused (ambient) activity while the radio itself is playing – the preparation of a meal during a radio play for example.'

With time running out I made a trip to the south coast to see the last week of an exhibition at the De La Warr Pavilion in Bexhill-on -Sea. The Pavilion, a Modernist icon right on the sea-front, is in itself worth the journey. It was named after the 9th Earl De La Warr, an interesting man who instigated the project and was mayor of the town in 1934 when the building was completed (he was also the first hereditary peer to join the Labour Party). Emigré architects Erich Mendelson and Serge Chermayeff designed the building which was listed Grade One in 2005 after years of neglect and refurbished to its present impressive state. It looks at its best on a clear sunny day but I took this photo of it in the overcast mid-January light to give you at least an idea of the place.

The exhibition I was there to see was *Keep Things As They Are,* a retrospective of the work of artist, writer and film-maker Ian Breakwell. I worked with Ian on and off over the years, from the early 1980s up until 2002 three years before he died. One of his on-going projects was his *Continuous Diary* which took many forms, being made up of paintings, photographs and texts in books and magazines. There was also a series of films of these diary entries, poignant funny/sad observations from everyday life, commissioned by Channel Four shortly after it started broadcasting in 1982. I filmed lots of these episodes with Ian as writer/presenter and our mutual friend, Anna Ridley, producing (you remember Anna produced *Another Way of Telling* for us too). The 'Diary' films were shown generally as the last programme of the day's television, after the religious Epilogue and before close-down. It's hard to imagine now a time when television felt the need for a religious homily to go with your bedtime cocoa and then actually shut down for the night. As the last broadcast programme Ian's films could be of any length and were usually around the 4-5 minutes mark with the longest one, if I remember correctly, running at 12 minutes, a film very critical of the Falklands War, and handed in to C4 by Anna at the last minute before transmission to avoid any censorship of the contents.

The main point of my journey to Ian's exhibition though was to watch *The Other Side*, a rarely-seen video installation which I shot for him at the De La Warr in 2002. It is a very moving 13 minute piece that transcends it's component parts.

Filmed from the top landing of the elegant staircase looking out towards the sea, the camera tracks slowly from side to side, parallel to the action, focussing on a group of elderly couples dancing around the outside of the topmost semi-circular balcony of the Pavilion to the sound of the sea and Schubert's Nocturne in E flat Major. Behind them is the backdrop of the late afternoon sky, beach and sea. The wind catches the dancers' hair and clothes as they waltz in slow-motion, seagulls cross the frame, people walk along the seafront in the distance and you glimpse the red 'no bathing' flag fluttering every now and then.

Between the dancers and the camera the vertical stairwell light crosses frame continuously as the camera tracks slowly left and right and the lens follows the couples, sometimes in a wide shot with the chrome hand-rail of the stairs in foreground, sometimes in close-up as they dance and turn in each other's arms. After 13 minutes the screen fades to black and there is the sound of glass shattering (an audio reference to vandalism in this rather rundown seaside town) followed by the loud cry of seagulls startled by the noise. The elegiac mood of the piece is broken sharply. Then, after a short pause the screen fades up once more to the original tracking shot and the whole sequence begins again.

The installation, and this is why it is not seen often, uses a large double-sided screen (16ft x 9ft) which runs diagonally across a darkened space with access all round for the audience. The images are projected on both sides of the screen and differ from each other in that the dancers feature mainly on one side while the other side shows predominately the same tracking shot but empty, the dancers absent. The Schubert Nocturne fills the dark space. I watched the installation four times through, sometimes lost in the piece itself but also occasionally thinking about the making of it, the component parts that Ian put together with the help of the editor in such a magical way. The dancers were all local people who came to the tea dances every week. During the filming they waltzed on the chilly balcony, not to Schubert but to a rather cheesy CD of popular waltzes played on a theatre organ.

My work on the camera was fairly straightforward although I recall struggling a little to maintain the visual continuity as later in the afternoon the winter sun began to set and the light levels changed, silhouetting the dancers against the horizon.

It was during his residency in 2000/01 at the De La Warr that Ian began to formulate the piece. He describes in an interview watching the dancing on the Pavilion terrace...'elderly people would get up out of their deck-chairs with great difficulty and the music propels them along and they begin to glide. There is something incredibly moving and dignified about these elderly people who suddenly become graceful. And if it is two women dancing together there is a sadness to it as well because they'll probably both be widows. I began to think of a kind of dance in the fading light from sunset through to darkness.'

Ian was also obsessed with characters who live on the margins of society through either choice or bad luck. He felt that we were all only one or two chance turns of fate away from that margin. It was the subject of several of the films I shot for him. I never found it very easy filming people who were down on their luck and homeless because to catch the reality of a situation that can easily be seen by a quick glance of the eye is difficult when that glance has to be translated into the direct stare of the camera lens. Just the small courtesy of asking permission often risked the moment slipping away.

I've been rather preoccupied at the moment preparing for an exhibition in April of new pastel works on paper. They are non-figurative images of overlapping planes of colour with elements of geometry too but not in the sense of mathematical geometry. Some were based initially on the visual devices used in 'Dazzle' camouflage to disguise shapes but as I'm not trying to hide anything in that practical sense they are used now by me to play off those beautiful, strong, dry colours that only pastel produces. It's quite a laborious process, which I won't go into here, because the coloured powder of the pastels is hard to control in this hard-edge way that I'm using it and the works often technically fail and I have to start again from scratch.

I am surrounded here by Nature with a capital 'N' but have chosen in these works from the last twelve months to turn my back on the world outside the studio (my worktable physically faces away from the view), by occupying myself with questions of colour and shape. *Not Nature* was going to be my title for the exhibition but it was thought to be too negative, although I didn't mean it in a negative way only as a helpful definition of what the pictures were not about. I have been asking myself why I chose to take this direction away from the examples of Nature? Perhaps, besides being fascinated with the non-figurative work I'm doing at the moment, it's because I'm surrounded by something that I feel I cannot improve upon or represent in any way satisfactory to myself? Last year I stood listening to a bird singing in the hedge. It was a riveting, virtuoso performance that went on for quite a time, a complex, brilliantly inventive song that, had I been a composer, could have had the effect of making me feel hopelessly ill-equipped. Last weekend at one of the events celebrating Benjamin Britten's centenary I listened to a sound recording of birds singing in his garden and I heard the song again – it was a nightingale.

In this quote Olivier Messiaen (who knew a thing or two about birdsong and whose music I love) brings together Nature and some of the things I've been trying to talk about:

'.. music is a part of time, a fraction of time, as is our own life, and that Nature, ever beautiful, ever great, ever new, Nature, an inextinguishable treasure-house of sounds and colours, forms and rhythms, the unequalled model for total developments and perpetual variation, that Nature is the supreme resource.'

I look forward to hearing from you
With love from us all
John

from John Berger March 2013

7/3/13.

Dear John,

I think of your exhibition coming up soon in April and you choosing which "dazzling" pastels to put in it. I like a lot the one you sent with your letter. It draws the spectator into itself because it is so multi-layered. The key-word is <u>overlap</u>: what one sees on top and what is hidden behind and the complexity between the two.

The plover which is called a lapwing is apparently so named because when it flies it changes from black to white, white to black, winking, opening and shutting, overlapping!

As a story-teller, Juan Muñoz was fascinated — even obsessed — by the co-existence of the everyday, the banal, with the mysterious, the incomprehensible. The oddity of the normal. What we take for granted overlaps something which is baffling; something which is wanting to be noticed beyond the edges or the borders of the overlap. And often in his work, I think, the baffling had to with time. Which is maybe why the assembly of Chinese relaxing during an interval is entitled "Many Times". And their lack of feet refers to what is baffling.

2.

Your film for Ian Breakwell's installation called "The Other Side" touches on something similar, no? Even the title could refer to the back of something which is overlapping something else. And furthermore there are the elderly dancers!

I remember going once to the guinguettes (the open-air cafés and dance-halls) on the banks of the Marne just outside Paris. Some were installed on the decks of old, anchored pleasure-boats. There were already installed there at the time of the Impressionists and ~~Renoir~~ Renoir painted couples dancing there. When we went, the couples were all elderly, from another period. I even have the souvenir (undoubtedly false) that all the women were wearing long dresses. What was unforgetable, however, was the transformation of these women and men when they got up from the tables and benches and, following the music, began to dance. They were no longer frail, hesitant or stooped and they became graceful, enchanted and poignant. And here too, as in the image you sent from your film, there was an overlapping: the time of the music overlapped the time of the present and the time of the past, fifty years earlier.

I remember that when I was a small kid – around four to six – I had a strong sense of Nature. I suspect most or all kids do. And then it's dismantled and taken to pieces by Reason, competitiveness and other priorities. Nature had the shape of an egg which surrounded you, everybody you knew and everything which happened to you.

I want to try to explain this better. It's very close to what Olivier Messiaen says in your quotation but it's a little more geometric or spatial.

The egg of Nature was immense and contained everything that existed. I thought of it as an egg because it was a container without corners. Outside it there was nothing. Nothing.

Most of what was inside was invisible and nameless but nevertheless very present. As present as your own two feet or your teeth. What you observed of Nature was inside the egg and visible. An avenue of trees. A horse. A carrot. The moon. A river. Each of these visible things had behind it countless invisible things to which it was related. More than that: it was the chosen messenger or sign of the invisible things that were behind it, that were crowding and bustling behind it.

The parentage between the visible thing and its invisible and mysterious "followers" was physical not symbolic. For example, carrot might have been an envoy of redness, pointedness, root, sand, badger, filigree leaves, rain, a taste that goes to the roof of the mouth, penetration. Both the uniqueness and the eloquence of a carrot depended for me on all its connections and overlappings which I could sense (with all five senses) but not identify or name.

This painting by Chagall suggests somewhat what the interior of the eggs is like.

And, as you may have guessed, all this is a way of suggesting that you might call your pastels exhibition <u>Overlappings</u>!

With love to you all

and the birds

John.

P.S. We put biscuits in a bowl on the floor of the stable for Nevo, the cat. He eats them but so also does a hedgehog. I often see him there nibbling. At first he scurried away, but now he's not alarmed and he goes on eating. They are such strange-looking animals. As if they live not on the ground but in a story ... Their "quills" are like sentences. And if books had feet and legs they'd be like those of a hedgehog. Maybe we should rename the stable a library? Did Dürer ever draw a hedgehog? I can see his drawing!

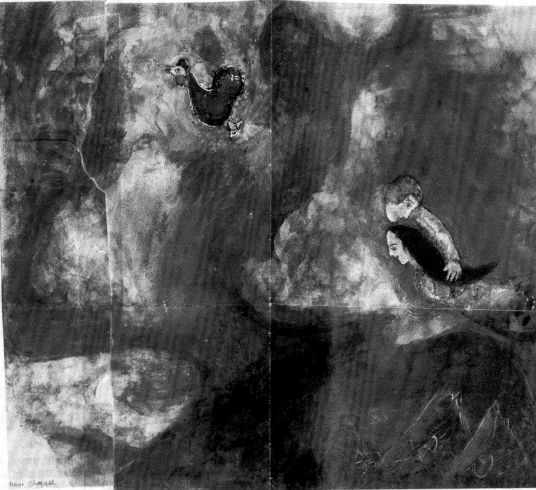

imported : Varian Fry accomplit le travail nécessaire pour rendre l'exil, sinon heureux, du moins possible. Il sauva en outre l'artiste du pire.

La grande traversée

Marc s'était en effet installé provisoirement avec Bella à Marseille, à l'*Hôtel Moderne*. Le 9 avril, il est victime d'une rafle, Bella s'affole. Fry prend son téléphone et règle habilement l'affaire. Un mois plus tard, le couple transite par Madrid avant d'arriver à Lisbonne, dans l'attente de la traversée vers New York. Le peintre ne touche plus à ses pinceaux ; ses personnages, il les a devant les yeux : «Dans le port, autour du navire, je retrouve ici des centaines de mes Juifs à baluchon. Un créateur et ses créatures prenant le même bateau : je n'ai jamais rien vu d'aussi triste.»

À New York, Chagall va peu à peu renouer les fils de sa vie, de sa sociabilité, de sa carrière. Il demeurera toujours nostalgique, habité par les souvenirs de la Russie et de la France, certes, et ne parlant guère l'anglais, mais il sait gré aux États-Unis de l'accueillir. Surtout, après quelques semaines de très vives angoisses, il

Dear John

I think of your exhibition coming up soon in April and you choosing which 'dazzling' pastels to put in it. I like a lot the one you sent with your letter. It draws the spectator into itself because it is so multi-layered. The key-word is overlap: what one sees on top and what is hidden behind and the complicity between the two.

The plover which is called a lapwing is apparently so named because when it flies it changes from black to white, white to black, winking, opening and shutting, overlapping!

As a story-teller Juan Muñoz was fascinated – even obsessed – by the co-existence of the everyday, the banal, with the mysterious, the incomprehensible. The oddity of the normal. What we take for granted overlaps something which is baffling; something which is waiting to be noticed beyond the edges or borders of the overlap. And often in his work, I think, the baffling had to do with time. Which is maybe why the assembly of Chinese relaxing during an interval is entitled *Many Times*. And their lack of feet refers to what is baffling.

Your film for Ian Breakwell's installation called *The Other Side* touches on something similar, no? Even the title could refer to the back of something which is overlapping something else. And furthermore there are the elderly dancers!

I remember once going to the guinguettes (the open-air cafés and dance-halls) on the banks of the Marne just outside Paris. Some were installed on the decks of old, anchored pleasure-boats. They were already installed there at the time of the Impressionists and Renoir painted couples dancing there. When we went the couples were all elderly, from another period. I even have the souvenir (undoubtedly false) that all the women were wearing long dresses. What was unforgettable, however, was the transformation of these women and men when they got up from the tables and benches, and following the music, began to dance. They were no longer frail, hesitant or stooped and they became graceful, enchanted and plangent. And here too, as in the image you sent from your film, there was an overlapping: the time of the music overlapped the time of the present and the time of the past, fifty years earlier.

I remember that when I was a small kid – around four to six – I had a strong sense of Nature. I suspect most or all kids do. And then it is dismantled and taken to pieces by Reason, competitiveness and other priorities. Nature had the shape of an egg which surrounded you, everybody you knew and everything which happened to you.

I want to try to explain this better. It's very close to what Olivier Messiaen says in your quotation but it's a little more geometric or spatial.

The egg of Nature was immense and contained everything that existed. I thought of it as an egg because it was a container without corners. Outside it there was nothing. Nothing.

Most of what was inside was invisible and nameless but nevertheless very present. As present as your own two feet or your teeth.

What you observed of Nature was inside the egg and visible. An avenue of trees. A horse. A carrot. The moon. A river. Each of these visible things had behind it countless invisible things to which it was related. More than that: it was the chosen messenger or sign of the invisible things that were behind it, that were crowding and bustling behind it.

The parentage between the visible thing and its invisible and mysterious 'followers' was physical not symbolic. For example, carrot might have been an envoy of redness, pointedness, root, sand, badger, filigree leaves, rain, a taste that goes to the roof of the mouth, penetration. Both the uniqueness and the eloquence of a carrot depended for me on all its connections and overlappings which I could sense (with all five senses) but not identify or name.

This painting by Chagall suggests somewhat what the interior of the egg is like.

And, as you may have guessed, all this is a way of suggesting that you might call your pastels exhibition Overlappings!

With love to you all and the birds
John

P.S. We put biscuits in a bowl on the floor of the stable for Nero, the cat. He eats them but so also does a hedgehog. I often see him there nibbling. At first he scurried away, but now he's not alarmed and he goes on eating. They are such strange-looking animals. As if they live not on the ground but in a story... Their 'quills' are like sentences. And if books had feet and legs they'd be like those of a hedgehog. Maybe we should rename the stable a library? Did Dürer ever draw a hedgehog? I can see his drawing!

from John Christie June 2013

Regarding Angels

Angels are messengers... It is said that they move through space at the speed of their own thoughts.

Michel Serres

Dear John

I'm not sure if Dürer ever drew a hedgehog but in
the process of trying to discover if he had I found
this small work on velum by his follower Hans
Hoffmann.
It was made fifty or so years after Dürer's famous
watercolour of a hare and stylistically the two are
closely connected. In both pictures the hare and
the hedgehog are shown against a similar neutral
background, separated from Nature as if to underline
the fact that the painter is the creator. In the
case of the hare this isolation from the natural
world is reinforced by the reflection of Dürer's
studio window in the creature's eye.
Hoffmann seems to have gone one better in claiming
the hedgehog for his own. I haven't examined the
original under a magnifying glass, it's in the Met
in New York, but from a catalogue reproduction it
looks as though he has included in his watercolour,
in the animal's eye, an image of himself at his
easel as if reflected in a convex mirror.

When I was a boy I had a pet hedgehog. It was a
young animal which, I seem to remember, my
brother and I easily caught in the grass beside a
footpath. We were with my mum and making our way
across the fields to Wickford station after a
weekend at my grandad's smallholding in Essex.
We brought the hedgehog back to our garden in
West Ham and named it Norman after the prickly
comedian Norman Wisdom. It seemed at first that
Norman (or maybe it should have been Norma, we
didn't check) was content to live in the city but
one day, while we were at school he squeezed
through a hole in the fence and disappeared.

Hoffmann's hedgehog looks as though he is just about to
do the same, alert and wary, waiting patiently for

Hans Hoffmann 'A Hedgehog' (before 1584)

his chance, once the artist is occupied elsewhere,
to quietly make a break for it back to nature.

Around the barn the fields have changed again
recently with the improvement in the weather.
I love the sight of that earlier, deep ploughing
which gives the land the appearance of a choppy
sea. Then weeks later the next phase when the harrow
breaks down the clods and a kind of calmness and
order settles on the landscape, waiting for the
newly-sown crops to start pushing through.

Here is a short list of things noticed on a recent
walk: red-breasted bullfinches nesting in the
hedgerow; the brief sound of a cuckoo from the wood
then a muntjac standing still at the entrance to
one of the paths watching me as I walk past; a
hawk, which I've only seen briefly so couldn't
accurately identify, seems to have taken up
residence in our empty owl box.

A few days ago I was in Southwold taking photos of
a friend's sculpture. It had even been warm enough
to have a picnic lunch on the beach and on my way
home I decided to call in to Holy Trinity at
Blythburgh. This is one of the most famous churches
in Suffolk. It is known as 'the Cathedral of the
Marshes' and sits on high ground above the river
Blyth overlooking to the east the estuary which
leads to Southwold and the North Sea. Peter Sager,
a German travel writer who wrote one of the most
enjoyable guide books to East Anglia, described it
as looking 'like an anchored ship stranded by the
retreating tide'. I read again Sebald's *Rings of
Saturn*, another German fascinated by the area, to
see if his route from the Sailor's Mission in
Southwold had taken him via Holy Trinity. But no, he
surprisingly doesn't mention visiting it on his way
south to Dunwich although he must have passed by.

One of the glories of the interior of Holy Trinity
is the painted roof with its twelve wooden angels
hovering above the nave. There was nobody around
when I arrived at about 5pm and the low sun was
streaming in through the clerestory, throwing a
lovely reflected light upwards onto the ceiling. I
lay on my back on the floor of the central aisle
and took several pictures of the angels directly
above me. Are they meant to give the impression of
floating, weightless in mid-air protecting the
congregation or are they supporting the roof with
their outstretched wings? It is hard to tell but
given that the figures were created in the mid-1400s
when people regarded angels as real beings perhaps
the answer is both.

There are various stories about these angels and
their survival over the years; one being that at
the beginning of April 1644, during the English
Civil War, William Dowsing a puritan soldier and

iconoclast inspected Holy Trinity and made a list of items in the church that had to be removed or destroyed under parliamentary order. The angels in the roof were on this list but, being too difficult to reach from the ground, remained in place despite being shot at with muskets by Dowsing and his aides in an attempt to dislodge them. When the angels were taken down during restoration in the 1970s the lead shot embedded in the carvings was found to be from the 18th century, a hundred years or so after Dowsing's visit, and an entry in the churchwarden's accounts from that time states that men were paid to shoot jackdaws nesting inside the church. Not such a good story as fervent puritans blasting away with guns at wooden angels 50 feet above them, but killing jackdaws is still an odd event to take place inside a church.

Lying there for a while under the angels it was hard to imagine this peaceful space being used as a shooting gallery, and thinking about the experience later that evening the time spent gazing up at Blythburgh's roof brought to mind a passage by Rousseau in his *Reveries of the Solitary Walker*. In the 'Fifth Walk', he describes his two-month stay in 1765 on the lake island of Saint-Pierre, Switzerland and writes how he would:

'...slip away and then procure a boat, in which I would row out to the middle of the lake where the water was calm. There I would stretch out in the bottom of the boat, gazing at the sky and allowing myself to drift slowly on the water, sometimes for several hours at a time, sunk into a thousand chaotic but delicious reveries, which, while they had no particular abiding object, were a hundred times more to my liking than the sweetest things I had ever experienced in what people choose to call the pleasures of life.'

Just over ten years ago I had the luck to travel
to Ethiopia, to make a film for the children's
charity PLAN. It was a trip full of very vivid
experiences and it seemed at times that I met
there people who could be described as angels.
One such pair were local nurses in Addis Ababa,
part of a team funded by the charity who looked
after women and girls in the poorer parts of the
capital suffering from Aids. I followed and
recorded them on their daily round of visits. I
remember one patient, a young woman in her twenties,
although she looked like an old lady, whose bed
was in a tiny corrugated iron room in the corner
of her family compound. It was hot and dark in
the dirt-floored space but the open door let in
enough daylight to see that the walls were covered
with newspaper pasted onto the tin as decoration.
The young woman herself was a rather pitiful
sight because you knew, without expensive drugs,
her condition would never stabilise or improve,
only get worse. But the two nurses treated her
with such tenderness and care that their visit
must have made a difference as they talked to her
quietly, changed her dressings and massaged her
arms and back in an effort to make her comfortable.

Later in the trip I travelled to the country region
around Lalibela, an arid and mountainous place,
about an hour's flight from Addis. There I filmed
school and agricultural projects supported by
PLAN. Selfishly what I was hoping for was a chance
on one of the days to see the cluster of early
Christian churches, the World Heritage Site, at
Lalibela. This complex of eleven buildings, three
separate groups a few hundred metres apart, are
carved from the solid rock. The buildings are
actually inside the red stone of the landscape.
Each church cut from the living rock on the orders
of King Lalibala at about the same time (around

1200) when in England great cathedrals like Lincoln
were being constructed. Except at Lincoln the
masons were building upwards towards the light in
an effort to reach closer to heaven. At Lalibela
the opposite was true, the workers burrowed down
into the stone, carving first the solid image of
the church and then cutting in through the windows
and doors to mine out the interior.

Here is a photo I took of the church of George
which stands on its own away from the main group,
a cruciform cut 10 metres down into the rock. It is
by no means the largest of the churches but it
was the one I was most drawn to. Perhaps because
it is such a direct and unambiguous statement of
purpose whereas the groups of buildings have a
complexity that somehow makes you forget the wonder
of how they were made. Overall it is a breathtaking

place and one of the young men from PLAN took me round the site on the last full day before I was due to fly back home. He spoke very good English and had been trained as a guide so was very knowledgeable about the historical aspects of the place. But I underestimated the strength of his faith in face of the facts when I remarked on the sheer scale of the work that had been achieved by the King's workforce when they only had rather primitive tools to hand. He told me that men had done some of the work but the bulk of it had been carried out by angels working throughout the night while the men slept. Thinking that he was relating a folk tale and wasn't being entirely serious I asked him how the men could get any rest with the noise of angels chipping away in the dark. He answered that it was because the angels worked very quietly. I stopped asking facetious questions then because he obviously believed that that was what had happened and who was I to doubt him.

In a 15th-century manuscript about the life of King Lalibala it was noted that 'Every Ethiopian who, having heard talk of these churches hewn from a single rock, and who does not make the pilgrimage to the holy city, is like a man with no desire to gaze on the face of Our Lord.'

Standing on the edge of the hole with the church of George laid out below me, my feet on the same level as the building's roof rising in the centre, I was given a view of the church quite unlike that of, say, Lincoln Cathedral where you gaze up at the stone structure soaring above you, defying gravity. In Lalibela you are floating above the church, looking down from an angel's point of view and marvelling at the industry of men and what they'd carved in the name of their faith – and the orders of their King.

I saw Markéta two weeks ago in London at the
opening of a show of her carnival photos. She has
that skill that the very best photographers have
of making herself invisible or perhaps making you
believe that she is absent from the scene when all
the time she is there and paying very close
attention to what's going on. She even seemed to
manage to do that at her own private view, one
minute talking and mixing with the crowd in the
gallery the next quietly gone from the room without
anyone spotting that she was missing.

One of my favourite photos of hers is this one
which you know well from her *Pilgrims* series, the
sleeping man taken in 1967 in Slovakia. I remember
Markéta told me that because of the noise made by
the pilgrims praying throughout the night inside
the church it was very difficult to get any sleep
so some slept out in the open, in the churchyard.

This man, photographed in the early dawn dressed
and ready to move off, is taking the opportunity
for a last snooze before the next leg of the
pilgrimage.

It is such a moving image; the polished leather
boots, the rough cloth suit, the backpack (looking
like a briefcase) held by string over his shoulder,
his legs already bent as though stepping forward
and his hands relaxed, one cushioning his head
against the base of the tree and the other lightly
resting on his thigh. Is he sleeping or listening
quietly to something nobody else can hear? He
could be an angel fallen to earth?

I found these words by Michel Serres that maybe indicates another way of experiencing the presence of angels beyond visible acts of human kindness.

'In the most ancient traditions, messenger-angels don't necessarily take on only human form; they may pass by in a breeze or a ruffling of the water, or in the heat and light of the sun and stars – in short, in any of the elementary fluxes and movements that make up our Earth.'

In a corner of my studio amongst the books and papers I have a plaster copy of William Blake's 1823 life mask. It wasn't a pleasant experience by all accounts to have the mask made and you can see his face is rather severe, buttoned up. In real life I imagine him to have had an open, friendly face. I recall a story of how Blake would walk, sometimes accompanied by Samuel Palmer, every Sunday from his home in Fountains Court on the Strand up to Hampstead Heath to visit his patron and friend, the painter John Linnell. The Linnell children would watch from a high window to catch the first glimpse of Blake coming across the heath and rush out to meet him. During the day he would read them stories and they later remembered from those visits his 'kind and gentle manner'.

I often put my hand on his forehead when I first come into the studio, a way of saying hello – Blake was someone with a direct link to the angels.

Wouldn't it have been interesting to have had a recording of William Blake's actual voice!

Love from us all in Suffolk

John

'Angels are messengers... It is said that they move through space at the speed of their own thoughts.'
Michel Serres

Dear John

I'm not sure if Dürer ever drew a hedgehog but in the process of trying to discover if he had I found this small work on velum by his follower Hans Hoffmann.

It was made fifty or so years after Dürer's famous watercolour of a hare and stylistically the two are closely connected. In both pictures the hare and the hedgehog are shown against a similar neutral background, separated from Nature as if to underline the fact that the painter is the creator. In the case of the hare this isolation from the natural world is reinforced by the reflection of Dürer's studio window in the creature's eye.

Hoffmann seems to have gone one better in claiming the hedgehog for his own. I haven't examined the original under a magnifying glass, it's in the Met in New York, but from a catalogue reproduction it looks as though he has included in his watercolour, in the animal's eye, an image of himself at his easel as if reflected in a convex mirror.

When I was a boy I had a pet hedgehog. It was a young animal which, I seem to remember, my brother and I easily caught in the grass beside a footpath. We were with my mum and making our way across the fields to Wickford station after a weekend at my grandad's smallholding in Essex. We brought the hedgehog back to our garden in West Ham and named it Norman after the prickly comedian Norman Wisdom. It seemed at first that Norman (or maybe it should have been Norma, we didn't check) was content to live in the city but one day, while we were at school he squeezed through a hole in the fence and disappeared.

Hoffmann's hedgehog looks as though he is just about to do the same, alert and wary, waiting patiently for his chance, once the artist is occupied elsewhere, to quietly make a break for it back to nature.

Around the barn the fields have changed again recently with the improvement in the weather. I love the sight of that earlier, deep ploughing which gives the land the appearance of a choppy sea. Then weeks later the next phase when the harrow breaks down the clods and a kind of calmness and order settles on the landscape, waiting for the newly-sown crops to start pushing through.

Here is a short list of things noticed on a recent walk:
red-breasted bullfinches nesting in the hedgerow; the brief sound of a cuckoo from the wood then a muntjac standing still at the entrance to one of the paths watching me as I walk past; a hawk, which I've only seen briefly so couldn't accurately identify, seems to have taken up residence in our empty owl box.

A few days ago I was in Southwold taking photos of a friend's sculpture,. It had even been warm enough to have a picnic lunch on the beach and on my way home I decided to call in to Holy Trinity at Blythburgh. This is one of the most famous churches in Suffolk. It is known as 'the Cathedral of the Marshes' and sits on high ground above the river Blyth overlooking to the east the estuary which leads to Southwold and the North Sea. Peter Sager, a German travel writer who wrote one of the most enjoyable guide books to East Anglia, described it as looking 'like an anchored ship stranded by the retreating tide'. I read again Sebald's *Rings of Saturn*, another German fascinated by the area, to see if his route from the Sailor's Mission in Southwold had taken him via Holy Trinity. But no, he surprisingly doesn't mention visiting it on his way south to Dunwich although he must have passed by.

One of the glories of the interior of Holy Trinity is the painted roof with its twelve wooden angels hovering above the nave. There was nobody around when I arrived at about 5pm and the low sun was streaming in through the clerestory, throwing a lovely reflected light upwards onto the ceiling. I lay on my back on the floor of the central aisle and took several pictures of the angels directly above me. Are they meant to give the impression of floating, weightless in mid-air protecting the congregation or are they supporting the roof with their outstretched wings? It is hard to tell but given that the figures were created in the mid 1400s when people regarded angels as real beings perhaps the answer is both.

There are various stories about these angels and their survival over the years; one being that at the beginning of April 1644, during the English Civil War, William Dowsing a puritan soldier and iconoclast inspected Holy Trinity and made a list of items in the church that had to be removed or destroyed under parliamentary order. The angels in the roof were on this list but, being too difficult to reach from the ground, remained in place despite being shot at with muskets by Dowsing and his aides in an attempt to dislodge them. When the angels were taken down during restoration in the 1970s the lead shot embedded in the carvings was found to be from the 18th century, a hundred years or so after Dowsing's visit, and an entry in the churchwarden's accounts from that time states that men were paid to shoot jackdaws nesting inside the church. Not such a good story as fervent puritans blasting away with guns at wooden angels 50 feet above them, but killing jackdaws is still an odd event to take place inside a church.

Lying there for a while under the angels it was hard to imagine this peaceful space being used as a shooting gallery, and thinking about the experience later that evening the time spent gazing up at Blythburgh's roof brought to mind a passage by Rousseau in his *Reveries of the Solitary Walker*. In the 'Fifth Walk', he describes his two-month stay in 1765 on the lake island of Saint-Pierre, Switzerland and writes how he would:

'...slip away and then procure a boat, in which I would row out to the middle of the lake where the water was calm. There I would stretch out in the bottom of the boat, gazing at the sky and allowing myself to drift slowly on the water, sometimes for several hours at a time, sunk into a thousand chaotic but delicious reveries, which, while they had no particular abiding object, were a hundred times more to my liking than the sweetest things I had ever experienced in what people choose to call the pleasures of life.'

Just over ten years ago I had the luck to travel to Ethiopia, to make a film for the children's charity PLAN. It was a trip full of very vivid experiences and it seemed at times that I met there people who could be described as angels. One such pair were local nurses in Addis Ababa, part of a team funded by the charity who looked after women and girls in the poorer parts of the capital suffering from Aids. I followed and recorded them on their daily round of visits. I remember one patient, a young woman in her twenties although she looked like an old lady, whose bed was in a tiny corrugated iron room in the corner of her family compound. It was hot and dark in the dirt-floored space but the open door let in enough daylight to see that the walls were covered with newspaper pasted onto the tin as decoration. The young woman herself was a rather pitiful sight because you knew, without expensive drugs, her condition would never stabilise or improve, only get worse. But the two nurses treated her with such tenderness and care that their visit must have made a difference as they talked to her quietly, changed her dressings and massaged her arms and back in an effort to make her comfortable.

Later in the trip I travelled to the country region around Lalibela, an arid and mountainous place, about an hour's flight from Addis. There I filmed school and agricultural projects supported by PLAN. Selfishly what I was hoping for was a chance on one of the days to see the cluster of early Christian churches, the World Heritage Site, at Lalibela. This complex of eleven buildings, three separate groups a few hundred metres apart, are carved from the solid rock. The buildings are actually inside the red stone of the landscape. Each church cut from the living rock on the orders of King Lalibala at about the same time (around 1200) when in England great cathedrals like Lincoln were being constructed. Except at Lincoln the masons were building upwards towards the light in an effort to reach closer to heaven. At Lalibela the opposite was true, the workers burrowed down into the stone, carving first the solid image of the church and then cutting in through the windows and doors to mine out the interior.

Here is a photo I took of the church of George which stands on its own away from the main group, a cruciform cut 10 metres down into the rock. It is by no means the largest of the churches but it was the one I was most drawn to. Perhaps because it is such a direct and unambiguous statement of purpose whereas the groups of buildings have a complexity that somehow makes you forget the wonder of how they were made.

Overall it is a breathtaking place and one of the young men from PLAN took me round the site on the last full day before I was due to fly back home. He spoke very good English and had been trained as a guide so was very knowledgeable about the historical aspects of the place. But I underestimated the strength of his faith in face of the facts when I remarked on the sheer scale of the work that had been achieved by the King's workforce when they only had rather primitive tools to hand. He told me that men had done some of the work but the bulk of it had been carried out by angels working throughout the night while the men slept. Thinking that he was relating a folk tale and wasn't being entirely serious I asked him how the men could get any rest with the noise of angels chipping away in the dark. He answered that it was because the angels worked very quietly. I stopped asking facetious questions then because he obviously believed that that was what had happened and who was I to doubt him.

In a 15th century manuscript about the life of King Lalibala it was noted that 'Every Ethiopian who, having heard talk of these churches hewn from a single rock, and who does not make the pilgrimage to the holy city, is like a man with no desire to gaze on the face of Our Lord.'

Standing on the edge of the hole with the church of George laid out below me, my feet on the same level as the building's roof rising in the centre, I was given a view of the church quite unlike that of, say, Lincoln Cathedral where you gaze up at the stone structure soaring above you, defying gravity. In Lalibela you are floating above the church, looking down from an angel's point of view and marvelling at the industry of men and what they'd carved in the name of their faith – and the orders of their King.

I saw Markéta (Luskačová) two weeks ago in London at the opening of a show of her carnival photos. She has that skill that the very best photographers have of making herself invisible or perhaps making you believe that she is absent from the scene when all the time she is there and paying very close attention to what's going on. She even seemed to manage to do that at her own private view, one minute talking and mixing with the crowd in the gallery the next quietly gone from the room without anyone spotting that she was missing.

One of my favourite photos of hers is this one which you know well from her *Pilgrims* series, the sleeping man taken in 1967 in Slovakia. I remember Markéta told me that because of the noise made by the pilgrims praying throughout the night inside the church it was very difficult to get any sleep so some slept out in the open, in the churchyard.

This man, photographed in the early dawn dressed and ready to move off, is taking the opportunity for a last snooze before the next leg of the pilgrimage.

It is such a moving image; the polished leather boots, the rough cloth suit, the backpack (looking like a briefcase) held by string over his shoulder, his legs already bent as though stepping forward and his hands relaxed, one cushioning his head against the base of the tree and the other lightly resting on his thigh. Is he sleeping or listening quietly to something nobody else can hear? He could be an angel fallen to earth?

I found these words by Michel Serres that maybe indicates another way of experiencing the presence of angels beyond visible acts of human kindness.

'In the most ancient traditions, messenger-angels don't necessarily take on only human form; they may pass by in a breeze or a ruffling of the water, or in the heat and light of the sun and stars – in short, in any of the elementary fluxes and movements that make up our Earth.'

In a corner of my studio amongst the books and papers I have a plaster copy of William Blake's 1823 life mask. It wasn't a pleasant experience by all accounts to have the mask made and you can see his face is rather severe, buttoned up. In real life I imagine him to have had an open, friendly face. I recall a story of how Blake would walk, sometimes accompanied by Samuel Palmer, every Sunday from his home in Fountains Court on the Strand up to Hampstead Heath to visit his patron and friend, the painter John

Linnell. The Linnell children would watch from a high window to catch the first glimpse of Blake coming across the heath and rush out to meet him. During the day he would read them stories and they later remembered from those visits his 'kind and gentle manner'.

I often put my hand on his forehead when I first come into the studio, a way of saying hello – Blake was someone with a direct link to the angels.

Wouldn't it have been interesting to have had a recording of William Blake's actual voice!

Love from us all in Suffolk
John

253

from John Berger October 2013

25/10/13.

Dear John,

When I read you I see your
barn as a kind of watch-tower, for
you observe so much from 'it and your
contact with the nature around you is
so patient and vivid . It's hard to
believe that you weren't brought-up in the
country — but maybe you were often with
your grandad near Wickford ? It's as
though you learnt to read nature (no
capital N!) before you learnt to read letters.

I love Hoffmann's hedgehog. There
on the floor, toes spread-out, waiting to
leave. I guess the folklore of
hedgehogs is similar across the world
wherever they live their discreet, mostly
hidden lives. There are their prickles
their don't-touch-me prickles, and, at the
same time, there is something gentle,
tender about them. It seems natural
to offer them a bowl of milk. They are
like an intimate secret, and it's their
spikes which guard the secret.

Angels! Are they messengers? ~~Do~~ Do
they form part of a divine hierarchy —
~ bureaucracy? — in the Kingdom of God?
I doubt it. It seems to me that they
are a very human invention. Creatures
from deep inside the human imagination.

They began, they begin with the
human recognition of the cruelty of life
and the ceaseless capacity of men to be
cruel. They are creatures born of our
recognition of our own vulnerability.

They have human bodies, either female or
male, yet they are invulnerable. They come
to guide and protect, and, above all, to
console us. They have none of the authority
of gods. Their approach is fraternal. They
are our equals in every respect, except
that they do not suffer. They hold and share
our suffering but are exempt from it. And
this is why they embody hope. The hope that
life can be different. Angels come into the
everyday world with a kind of contraband:
the contraband of immunity from pain and
the illumination of a painless world. Their
gift is not unlike that of certain drugs, but
it is gratuitous — one doesn't have to pay at
some other level.

Answers are provoked by questions, and angels are the answer to a form of human questioning. Not an answer coming from God but an answer coming from human perception, when pain is overcome or quiescent, but has not been forgotten, for as much as ~~they~~ angels embody hope, they also embody Pity.

Their bodies are androgynous and in the self-sufficiency which this implies there is a peacefulness which is synonomous with an openess. Angels are visitors, and, ~~at the same time~~ simultaneously, they are hosts offering, however briefly, succour and shelter.

I see you lying on your back in the aisle of the church in ~~Blythborough~~ Blythburgh taking your photos of the carved angels against the wooden roof, and, watching you, I smile and I want to add that angels, when they have'nt been recruited by the Church into the Divine bureaucracy, are never solemn. Saints are. Prophets are. But not angels. Perhaps this is connected with their wings. They defy gravity. They are quite close to the sensation that Rousseau describes so graphically in your quotation.

Marketa's photo of the sleeping pilgrim in Slovakia is unforgetable. The word composition as applied to an image takes on here a different meaning because everything here is composed like a song or music around what he is experiencing. For me he's not like an angel, but in his sleep or trance he's watching an angel who is watching over him.

Not long ago I was in a small town in the south of France and walking along the street one morning I came upon a family of tumblers or saltinbanques performing near a supermarket. A father, three boys, a girl and a dog, a scots terrier. The dog I later found out was called Hella and the father Massimio.

The eldest boy who was probably seventeen (difficult to estimate their ages because for them there is no category of childhood) was the principal juggler and handler.

The girl of six or seven climbed him as if he was a tree and he stood her on her head on his head. The father was standing behind them with an amplifier and sound gear on the paving stones between his feet. He was watching them with beagle eyes and strumming on a guitar.

Then comes the moment for David (ten or eleven years old) to do his number. There are only half a dozen spectators, it's midmorning, people are busy.

He gets on his unicycle, rides it down the street, turns and rides back with the very minimum of exertion. ~~they~~ He's just showing his credentials.

Then he dismounts on to the sidewalk where there is a stuffed leather ball, the size of a very large pumpkin. He kicks off his sneakers and steps on to the ball. With the soles of his feet taking on the curvature of the ball and pushing with his heels against the ball, he slowly persuades it forward and the two of them advance. He keeps both arms down by his side. Nothing he does reveals the difficulty of maintaining his balance on the rolling ~~the~~ ball.

He stands on it, chin up, looking into the far distance. And he begins to sing, accompanied by his father playing a mouth organ.

He sings in an unruffled tenor voice. The song is Sardinian and describes what happens when a jinx is put on you, a story as old as the hills.

Triumph and jinx.

Jinx and triumph brought together in an act which, as you listen and watch it on the street corner, you hope will never stop.

I felt then as if I was watching
an angel. After the angel vanished I
talked to David and the whole family and
we had a coffee together. The same evening
they were performing on the same site before
a passing public that was larger. The
father had the face of an old trainer of
athletes. They slept in a camping car.

Maybe angels do too?

What I'm trying to get at is
that angels, although they are used in
stories as messengers (and the word angel
derives from the Ancient Greek word for
messenger), belong to us who receive
the messages and to the Earth on which
we live. They are not heavenly bodies;
they are creatures of our own inner space ~~imagination~~ and
if they are employed to carry messages, they
are at the same time in themselves a
message from us to ourselves. A
message about consolation and determination.

Let's end on a light note. The lake
surrounded by mountains is deep and about
70 km long. On the southern side of the
lake is a town on a hill, and between the

hill and lakeside there is space for a small
harbour, a promenade with two cafés, a
modest swimming pool, a narrow shingle beach
and a grass bank with trees. On summer
days in August this miniature location
adds up to a minimal, improvised seaside
resort.

Those who gather there are on vacation.
They have left their everyday lives behind
somewhere. They have emptied themselves.
The etymological root of the word vacation
is the Latin Vacare : to be empty ... to
be free.

If you walk there, you have to pick
your way — for the grassy space is narrow
and very small — you have to pick your
way between their mostly reclining freedoms!
Barefoot, barelegged, lying on towels in
the sun or in the shade of the trees,
some swimming with kids, some lounging
in deck-chairs. No big projects, for the
place is too small and the time too short.
No deadlines. Few words. The world
and its vocabulary, which they normally
repeat but don't believe in, have been
left behind. To be empty, doing nothing.

Yet not quite. Little blessings arrive
which they collect. For the most part they

are memories, yet is it is misleading to say this, for, at the same time, they are promises. They collect the remembered pleasures of promises, which cannot apply to the future which they have gladly vacated, but somehow do apply to the brief, "empty" present.

The promises are wordless and physical. Some can be seen, some can be touched, others can be heard, some can be tasted. Some are no more than messages in the pulse.

The taste of chocolate. The width of her hips. The splashing of water. The length of the daughter's drenched hair. The way he laughed when he woke up this morning. The gulls above the lake. The dog with its tongue hanging out in the heat. The tattoo he made such a thing of. Such messages are wordless yet they are shareable with a few others who are in the know. They are all messages about a remembered expectancy, about an open but not guaranteed promise concerning life, about an expectancy which, when refound one sunny afternoon on vacation, acquires a physical presence -- like ~~an angel's~~ the presence of an angel.

With love to you all

John.

Dear John

When I read you I see your barn as a kind of watch-tower, for
you observe so much from it and your contact with the nature
around you is so patient and vivid. It's hard to believe you weren't
brought up in the country – but maybe you were often with your
grandad in Wickford? It's as though you learnt to read nature
(no capital N!) before you learnt to read letters.

I love Hoffmann's hedgehog. There on the floor, toes spread-out,
waiting to leave. I guess the folklore of hedgehogs is similar across
the world wherever they live their discreet, mostly hidden lives.
There are their prickles, their don't-touch-me prickles, and, at the
same time, there is something gentle, tender about them. It seems
natural to offer them a bowl of milk. They are like an intimate
secret, and it's their spikes which guard their secret.

Angels! Are they messengers? Do they form part of a divine
hierarchy – or bureaucracy – in the Kingdom of God? I doubt it.
It seems to me that they are a very human invention. Creatures
from deep inside the human imagination.

They began, they begin with the human recognition of the cruelty
of life and the ceaseless capacity of men to be cruel. They are
creatures born of our recognition of our own vulnerability.

They have human bodies, either female or male, yet they are
invulnerable. They come to guide and protect, and, above all, to
console us. They have none of the authority of gods. Their
approach is fraternal. They are our equals in every respect, except
that they do not suffer. They hold and share our suffering but are
exempt from it. And this is why they embrace hope. The hope
that life can be different. Angels come into the everyday world
with a kind of contraband: the contraband of immunity from pain
and the illumination of a painless world. Their gift is not unlike that
of certain drugs, but it is gratuitous – one doesn't have to pay at
some other level.

Answers are provoked by questions, and angels are the answer
to a form of human questioning. Not an answer coming from
God but an answer coming from human perception, when pain is
overcome or quiescent, but has not been forgotten, for as much
as angels embody hope, they also embody Pity.

Their bodies are androgynous and in the self-sufficiency which
this implies there is a peacefulness which is synonymous with an
openness. Angels are visitors, and, simultaneously, they are hosts
offering, however briefly, succour and shelter.

I see you lying on your back in the aisle of the church in Blythburgh
taking your photos of the carved angels against the wooden roof,
and, watching you, I smile and want to add that angels when they
haven't been recruited by the Church into the Divine bureaucracy,
are never solemn. Saints are. Prophets are. But not angels. Perhaps
this is connected with their wings. They defy gravity. They are quite
close to the sensation that Rousseau describes so graphically in
your quotation.

Markéta's photo of the sleeping pilgrim in Slovakia is unforgettable.
The word composition as applied to an image takes on here a

different meaning because everything here is composed like a song or music around what he is experiencing. For me he is not like and angel, but in his sleep or trance he's watching an angel who is watching over him.

Not long ago I was in a small town in the south of France and walking along the street one morning I came upon a family of tumblers or saltimbanques performing near a supermarket. A father, three boys, a girl and a dog, a Scots terrier. The dog I later found out was called Nella and the father Massimo.

The oldest boy who was probably seventeen (difficult to estimate their ages because for them there is no category of childhood) was the principal juggler and handler.

The girl of six or seven climbed him as if he was a tree and he stood her on her head on his head. The father was standing behind them with an amplifier and sound gear on the paving stones between his feet. He was watching them with beagle eyes and strumming on a guitar.

Then comes the moment for David (ten or eleven years old) to do his number. There are only half a dozen spectators, it's midmorning, people are busy.

He gets on his bicycle, rides it down the street, turns and rides back with the very minimum of exertion. He's just showing his credentials.

Then he dismounts on to the sidewalk where there is a stuffed leather ball, the size of a very large pumpkin. He kicks off his sneakers and steps on to the ball. With the soles of his feet taking on the curvature of the ball and pushing with his heels against the ball, he slowly persuades it forward and the two of them advance. He keeps both arms down by his side. Nothing he does reveals the difficulty of maintaining his balance on the rolling ball.

He stands on it, chin up, looking into the far distance. And he begins to sing, accompanied by his father playing a mouth organ. He sings in an unruffled tenor voice. The song is Sardinian and describes what happens when a jinx is put on you, a story as old as the hills.

Triumph and jinx.

Jinx and triumph brought together in an act which, as you listen and watch it on the street corner, you hope will never stop.

I felt then as if I was watching an angel. After the angel vanished I talked to David and the whole family and we had coffee together. The same evening they were performing on the same site before a passing public that was larger. The father had the face of an old trainer of athletes. They slept in a camping car.

Maybe angels do too?

What I am trying to get at is that angels, although they are used in stories as messengers (and the word angel derives from the Ancient Greek word for messenger), belong to us who receive the messages and to the Earth on which we live. they are not heavenly bodies; they are creatures of our own inner space, and if

they are employed to carry messages, they are at the same time in themselves a message from us to ourselves. A message about consolation and determination.

Let's end on a light note. The lake surrounded by mountains is deep and about 70km long. On the southern side of the lake is a town on a hill, and between the hill and lakeside there is space for a small harbour, a promenade with two cafés, a modest swimming pool, a narrow shingle beach and a grass bank with trees. On summer days in August this miniature location adds up to a minimal, improvised seaside resort.

Those who gather there are on vacation. They have left their everyday lives behind somewhere. They have emptied themselves. The etymological root of the word vacation is the Latin *vacave*: to empty...to be free.

If you walk there, you have to pick your way – for the grassy space is narrow and very small – you have to pick your way between their mostly reclining freedoms! Barefoot, barelegged, lying on towels in the sun or in the shade of the trees, some swimming with kids, some lounging in deck-chairs. No big projects, for the place is too small and the time too short. No deadlines. Few words. The world and its vocabulary, which they normally repeat but don't believe in, have been left behind. To be empty, doing nothing.

Yet not quite. Little blessings arrive which they collect. For the most part they are memories, yet it is misleading to say this, for, at the same time, they are promises. They collect the remembered pleasures of promises, which cannot apply to the future which they have gladly vacated, but somehow do apply to the brief, 'empty' present.

The promises are wordless and physical. Some can be seen, some can be touched, others can be heard, some can be tasted. Some are no more than messages in the pulse.

The taste of chocolate. The width of her hips. The splashing of water. The length of the daughter's drenched hair. The way he laughed when he woke up in the morning. The gulls above the lake. The dog with its tongue hanging out in the heat. The tattoo he made such a thing of. Such messages are wordless yet they are shareable with a few others who are in the know. They are all messages about a remembered expectancy, about an open but not guaranteed promise concerning life, about an expectancy which, when refound one sunny afternoon on vacation, acquired a physical presence – like the presence of an angel.

With love to you all

John

from John Christie January 2014

An atlas for the next life

'In my photographic work I was always especially entranced, said Austerlitz, by the moment when the shadows of reality, so to speak, emerge out of nothing on the exposed paper, as memories do in the middle of the night, darkening again if you try to cling to them, just like a photographic print left in the developing bath too long.'

W. G. Sebald – *Austerlitz*

Dear John

December and a very strong wind blowing in across
the fields. Walking up the hill with the wood to
my right the air was filled with leaves swirling
horizontally around me. The perimeter bushes are
now almost bare of foliage and you can see the
trees within the wood standing in a sea of fallen
leaves. The combination of wet grass underfoot
and the noise of the wind in the branches meant I
could for once walk without making a sound. There
were plenty of fresh mole hills and signs of
other burrows along the edges of the track but
apart from one or two birds far away in the sky
there was not another creature to be seen. Later
in the day I heard on the radio that these gale-
force winds combined with low atmospheric pressure
and the threat of surge tides had put the east
coast on high flood alert. Around midnight the
sea was expected to rise to its highest level for
over 60 years, higher than The Great Tide which
flooded large areas of the East Anglian coast in
January 1953 killing over 300 people. Next day in
Aldeburgh the noise of the North Sea dragging the
shingle away after each wave was louder than I'd
ever heard it, the water the same muddy colour as
the ploughed fields surrounding the wood. The
tide line showed that the sea had advanced up the
beach way beyond its usual level, reaching as far
as the low sea wall.

Sometimes Theo, who is eleven now, comes with me
on the footpath and because we tend to talk all the
time we often miss or frighten away any creatures
that are nearby. Although the wood is private I
have been in there a couple of times. The first
was seven years ago during the restoration of the
barn to select a tree with the correct curve in
its trunk to provide the timber for some missing
roof braces. I was told by the conservation officer
(the building is Grade 2 listed) that most of the

270

original braces had been taken out in Victorian times and replaced by oak shoulders to widen the interior and accommodate larger farm wagons. Our carpenter made a full-size (3m) plywood pattern from one of the remaining struts and we carried this template into the wood to place against suitable oaks until one was found with the right curvature so its natural grain would follow the arc of the brace. I counted 183 annual growth rings across the stump of the felled tree. The 19th-century shoulders had to be left in place as part of the history of the building but six new braces were sawn from the trunk and put back in position to restore the strength and visual balance of the roof.

Three of the new braces with one of the 19th C oak shoulders still in place.

Last autumn I was in the wood helping the woodcutter (he'd hurt his back) load up some logs for our winter firewood and he told me that only a few days previously he'd seen a large red deer with magnificent antlers watching him silently from the bushes close by. The two of them had stood observing each other for a minute or so before the deer, in its own good time, slipped away. It was an animal he'd not seen before in this area because they usually wander the lowland heaths nearer the coast. I'd never spotted a red deer around here either and was hoping that the other day, under cover of the noise of the gale perhaps, I might catch a glimpse of one in amongst the trees. It is more than likely that the deer has watched Theo and me at some point in the past as we walked by on the footpath deep in conversation.

Angels. Perhaps in the end I relate more to a cinema vision of them as in, for instance, Wim Wenders' *Wings of Desire* where he does away almost entirely with the convention of heavenly wings and dresses them in modern clothes, making his angels empathetic creatures rather than religious out-riders. I remember the soundtrack of distressed human thoughts that they are tuned in to (like a jumble of radio signals in the air), an audio version perhaps of Michel Serres' 'elemental fluxes and movements' of nature.

This recollection of the film and its circus artiste, Solveig Dommartin, with her theatrical costume wings brought back to me from somewhere in the back of my mind a vivid memory of seeing Victoria Chaplin perform, in the '70s, with *Le Cirque Imaginaire* at Riverside Studios, Hammersmith. Sitting, balanced on the trapeze, she swung higher and higher, way out over the audience. There was no safety net and she made the crowd gasp in horror when at the top of her swing above our heads she suddenly appeared to slip and fall. Skilfully she caught the bar behind her knees and, hanging upside down, repeatedly brushed, with her long dark hair, the faces of the people looking up at her.

I was going to include a quote from Rilke in the last letter because the *Duino Elegies* are full, from the beginning, with references to angels:

'Who, if I cried, would hear me from the angelic
      Orders?'

And later:

'For beauty is nothing but the beginning of terror which we are barely able to endure, and it amazes us so,
because it serenely disdains to destroy us.
Every angel is terrible.'

Did I want to think of beauty (or angels) in those terms? I wasn't sure then that I did which is why I originally left those quotations from Rilke out. Then some connections brought me back to him.

Your description of the jugglers reminded me of a painting or maybe more correctly the word 'saltimbanques' reminded me. The group on the left of Picasso's famous 1905 *Family of Saltimbanques* bears a resemblance to your performers – a father figure, three boys and a girl – although the father in your account wasn't as fat, I'm sure, as the older man in the painting or I think you might have mentioned it.

But the ages seemed right and as I tried to discover a bit more about the picture I checked in a book

which I hadn't opened for some time, *Picasso: His Life and Work* by Roland Penrose (it was a school prize I chose, the only one I ever recall getting).

In the book Penrose talks about the painting and reveals that Rilke wrote one of the *Duino Elegies* under its spell:

'The freshness with which the picture is painted contributes to the mystery of their presence. This mystery haunted the poet Rainer Maria Rilke when in 1914 he asked if he might live in the same room with "the great Picasso", which then belonged to Hertha von Koenig in Munich. Sharing Picasso's fascination for the wandering circus folk of Paris, he was inspired to write the fifth of his *Duino Elegies*, while living, he later told a friend, "with the loveliest Picasso (the Saltimbanques) in which there is so much Paris that for moments I forget". In these lines he speaks of the wandering players he had beside him:

'But tell me, who are they, these acrobats,
        even a little
more fleeting than we ourselves,.....'"

Recently in London one of the exhibitions I saw was
Daumier: Visions of Paris at the RA which contained
a small group of paintings of saltimbanques. Daumier's
wandering players are less fleeting than the
Picasso group and very much appear, as he painted them,
real characters existing on the margin of society.

On that stormy walk around the wood I thought about
an artist whose work I like very much, Hans Waanders.
Perhaps it was the absence of wildlife that brought
him into my mind. He was an artist obsessed by a
bird I recall only having ever glimpsed once many
years ago, the kingfisher.

Kingfisher porch, Empel, Nederland

Hans Waanders lived in The Netherlands and died, aged 50, in 2001. He left behind him a very single-minded body of work.

An entry in an exhibition catalogue mentions a chance encounter in his life that became decisive:

'On October the 4th 1982 he saw for the first time the kingfisher along the river Maas. From that moment collecting and working out information about this bird started. The tangible result of the longing to see the kingfisher again.'

I never met him unfortunately but I have a number of the beautiful books and postcards which he published in small editions and often hand stamped with images of the kingfisher printed from relief blocks he'd carved from ordinary pencil rubbers.

One of his books, *Perches* published around the time of his death features a series of photographs made in Holland, France, Germany and the UK. Each picture shows a stick or twig pushed into the mud, grasses or stones of a riverbank as an invitation to the kingfisher to return and perch above the water. The strong feelings of absence and also hope in each of these photos is very powerful.

On my most recent visit to the Sainsbury Centre two weeks ago there had been quite a change around, a rearrangement and upgrading of the downstairs galleries to accommodate a large survey exhibition. The reserve collection where I first came across Auerbach's drawing of Leon Kossoff has moved upstairs to the ground floor, which means that the works are now properly displayed and that hidden-away quality that I liked, the feeling

you were discovering a work that had been somehow
left behind, has been lost. The portrait of Kossoff
is in full view (as it should be) but now its
subject somehow appears more fixed, not so
fugitive. So the maps I made and the positions of
pictures I described in those first letters are
often no longer valid which is of course the
problem with maps, they only tell you how things
were at the time when the map was made.

You sent me, in one of the *Cadmium Red* letters, a
phrase – 'perhaps we could make a kind of atlas
for the next life'. It is an idea that has remained
with me and I've often asked myself how could one
make such an atlas? What did you mean by 'the
next life'? The afterlife? I didn't think so but
anyway that wasn't helpful because however
comforting the thoughts of an afterlife are it is
not something I really believe in anymore than I
believe in the existence of heavenly angels.
Maybe you meant the next phase of life like the
transition from the city to the countryside I
made eight years ago? Or perhaps you meant just
simply the next part of life, the part that is
constantly arriving and departing day by day and
the memory of which, like a map, becomes the trace
of activities and places left behind (I have a
picture in mind now of one of your map drawings
with the speeding motorcyclist). Perhaps over the
last three years what we've brought together in
these letters, with all their various memories and
experiences, is a collection of maps and pathways,
one possible version of the atlas you originally
suggested?

With Love
John

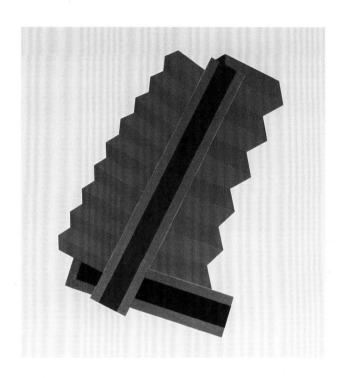

P.S. Here's one of a series of pastels I
made recently which came from
looking at a sculpture that we
talked about some time ago, your friend
Zadkine's 'The Accordion Player' — and
below part of a poem by Louis Zukofsky
— not sure if Einstein actually said
this but I hope he did.

'Everything should be as simple as it can be,
Says Einstein,
But not simpler'.

'In my photographic work I was always especially entranced, said Austerlitz, by the moment when the shadows of reality, so to speak, emerge out of nothing on the exposed paper, as memories do in the middle of the night, darkening again if you try to cling to them, just like a photographic print left in the developing bath too long.'
W.G. Sebald – *Austerlitz*

Dear John

December and a very strong wind blowing in across the fields. Walking up the hill with the wood to my right the air was filled with leaves swirling horizontally around me. The perimeter bushes are now almost bare of foliage and you can see the trees within the wood standing in a sea of fallen leaves. The combination of wet grass underfoot and the noise of the wind in the branches meant I could for once walk without making a sound. There were plenty of fresh mole hills and signs of other burrows along the edges of the track but apart from one or two birds far away in the sky there was not another creature to be seen. Later in the day I heard on the radio that these gale-force winds combined with low atmospheric pressure and the threat of surge tides had put the east coast on high flood alert. Around midnight the sea was expected to rise to its highest level for over 60 years, higher than The Great Tide which flooded large areas of the East Anglian coast in January 1953 killing over 300 people. Next day in Aldeburgh the noise of the North Sea dragging the shingle away after each wave was louder than I'd ever heard it, the water the same muddy colour as the ploughed fields surrounding the wood. The tide line showed that the sea had advanced up the beach way beyond its usual level, reaching as far as the low sea wall.

Sometimes Theo, who is eleven now, comes with me on the foot-path and because we tend to talk all the time we often miss or frighten away any creatures that are nearby. Although the wood is private I have been in there a couple of times. The first was seven years ago during the restoration of the barn to select a tree with the correct curve in its trunk to provide the timber for some missing roof braces. I was told by the conservation officer (the building is Grade 2 listed) that most of the original braces had been taken out in Victorian times and replaced by oak shoulders to widen the interior and accommodate larger farm wagons. Our carpenter made a full-size (3m) plywood pattern from one of the remaining struts and we carried this template into the wood to place against suitable oaks until one was found with the right curvature so its natural grain would follow the arc of the brace. I counted 183 annual growth rings across the stump of the felled tree. The 19th-century shoulders had to be left in place as part of the history of the building but six new braces were sawn from the trunk and put back in position to restore the strength and visual balance of the roof.

Last autumn I was in the wood helping the woodcutter (he'd hurt his back) load up some logs for our winter firewood and he told me that only a few days previously he'd seen a large red deer with magnificent antlers watching him silently from the bushes close by. The two of them had stood observing each other for a minute or so before the deer, in its own good time, slipped away. It was an animal he'd not seen before in this area because they usually wander the lowland heaths nearer the coast. I'd never

spotted a red deer around here either and was hoping that the other day, under cover of the noise of the gale perhaps, I might catch a glimpse of one in amongst the trees. It is more than likely that the deer has watched Theo and me at some point in the past as we walked by on the footpath deep in conversation.

Angels,. Perhaps in the end I relate more to a cinema vision of them as in, for instance, Wim Wenders' *Wings of Desire* where he does away almost entirely with the convention of heavenly wings and dresses them in modern clothes, making his angels empathetic creatures rather than religious outriders. I remember the soundtrack of distressed human thoughts that they are tuned in to (like a jumble of radio signals in the air), an audio version perhaps of Michel Serres' 'elemental fluxes and movements' of nature.

This recollection of the film and its circus artiste, Solveig Dommartin, with her theatrical costume wings brought back to me from somewhere in the back of my mind a vivid memory of seeing Victoria Chaplin perform, in the '70s, with *Le Cirque Imaginaire* at Riverside Studios, Hammersmith. Sitting, balanced on the trapeze, she swung higher and higher, way out over the audience. There was no safety net and she made the crowd gasp in horror when at the top of her swing above our heads she suddenly appeared to slip and fall. Skilfully she caught the bar behind her knees and, hanging upside down, repeatedly brushed, with her long dark hair, the faces of the people looking up at her.

I was going to include a quote from Rilke in the last letter because the *Duino Elegies* are full, from the beginning, with references to angels:

'Who, if I cried, would hear me from the angelic Orders?'

And later:

'For beauty is nothing but the beginning of terror
which we are barely able to endure, and it amazes us so,
because it serenely disdains to destroy us.
Every angel is terrible.'

Did I want to think of beauty (or angels) in those terms? I wasn't sure then that I did which is why I originally left those quotations from Rilke out. Then some connections brought me back to him.

Your description of the jugglers reminded me of a painting or maybe more correctly the word 'saltimbanques' reminded me. The group on the left of Picasso's famous 1905 *Family of Saltimbanques* bears a resemblance to your performers – a father figure, three boys and a girl – although the father in your account wasn't as fat, I'm sure, as the older man in the painting or I think you might have mentioned it. But the ages seemed right and as I tried to discover a bit more about the picture I checked in a book which I hadn't opened for some time, *Picasso: His Life and Work* by Roland Penrose (it was a school prize I chose, the only one I ever recall getting). In the book Penrose talks about the painting and reveals that Rilke wrote one of the *Duino Elegies* under its spell:

''The freshness with which the picture is painted contributes to the mystery of their presence. This mystery haunted the poet

Rainer Maria Rilke when in 1914 he asked if he might live in the same room with "the great Picasso", which then belonged to Hertha von Koenig in Munich. Sharing Picasso's fascination for the wandering circus folk of Paris, he was inspired to write the fifth of his *Duino Elegies*, while living, he later told a friend, "with the loveliest Picasso (the *Saltimbanques*) in which there is so much Paris that for moments I forget". In these lines he speaks of the wandering players he had beside him:
'But tell me, who are they, these acrobats,
even a little
more fleeting than we ourselves,.....'"

Recently in London one of the exhibitions I saw was *Daumier: Visions of Paris* at the Royal Academy which contained a small group of paintings of saltimbanques. Daumier's wandering players are less fleeting than the Picasso group and very much appear, as he painted them, real characters existing on the margin of society.

On that stormy walk around the wood I thought about an artist whose work I like very much, Hans Waanders. Perhaps it was the absence of wildlife that brought him into my mind. He was an artist obsessed by a bird I recall only having ever glimpsed once many years ago, the kingfisher.

Hans Waanders lived in The Netherlands and died, aged 50, in 2001. He left behind him a very single-minded body of work. An entry in an exhibition catalogue mentions a chance encounter in his life that became decisive:

'On October the 4th 1982 he saw for the first time the kingfisher along the river Maas. From that moment collecting and working out information about this bird started. The tangible result of the longing to see the kingfisher again.'

I never met him unfortunately but I have a number of the beautiful books and postcards which he published in small editions and often hand stamped with images of the kingfisher printed from relief blocks he'd carved from ordinary pencil rubbers.

One of his books, *Perches* published around the time of his death features a series of photographs made in Holland, France, Germany and the UK. Each picture shows a stick or twig pushed into the mud, grasses or stones of a riverbank as an invitation to the kingfisher to return and perch above the water. The strong feelings of absence and also hope in each of these photos is very powerful.

On my most recent visit to the Sainsbury Centre two weeks ago there had been quite a change around, a rearrangement and upgrading of the downstairs galleries to accommodate a large survey exhibition. The reserve collection where I first came across Auerbach's drawing of Leon Kossoff has moved upstairs to the ground floor, which means that the works are now properly displayed and that hidden-away quality that I liked, the feeling you were discovering a work that had been somehow left behind, has been lost. The portrait of Kossoff is in full view (as it should be) but now its subject somehow appears more fixed, not so fugitive. So the maps I made and the positions of pictures I described in those first letters are often no longer valid which is of course the problem with maps, they only tell you how things were at the time when the map was made.

You sent me, in one of the *Cadmium Red* letters, a phrase – 'perhaps we could make a kind of atlas for the next life'. It is an idea that has remained with me and I've often asked myself how could one make such an atlas? What did you mean by 'the next life'? The afterlife? I didn't think so but anyway that wasn't helpful because however comforting the thoughts of an afterlife are it is not something I really believe in anymore than I believe in the existence of heavenly angels.

Maybe you meant the next phase of life like the journey from the city to the countryside I made eight years ago? Or perhaps you meant just simply the next part of life, the part that is constantly arriving and departing day by day and which, like a map, becomes the trace of activities and places left behind (I have a picture in mind now of one of your map drawings with the speeding motor-cyclist). Perhaps over the last three years what we've brought together in these letters, with all their various memories and experiences, is a collection of maps and pathways, one possible version of the atlas you originally suggested?

With love
John

PS. Here's one of a series of pastels I made recently which came from looking at a sculpture that we talked about some time ago, your friend Zadkine's *The Accordion Player* and below, part of a poem by Louis Zukofsky – not sure if Einstein actually said this but I hope he did.

'Everything should be as simple as it can be,
Says Einstein
But not simpler.'

Destinez-moi la Palestine

Jardin de Sandra
Quincy - Haute-Savoie

Yes, as you say, why
not a map? And so one
can find one's way, like
our letters, from one
life to another!

I send you one

John.

Imprimerie Uberti-Jourdan - Bonneville - RC77B52

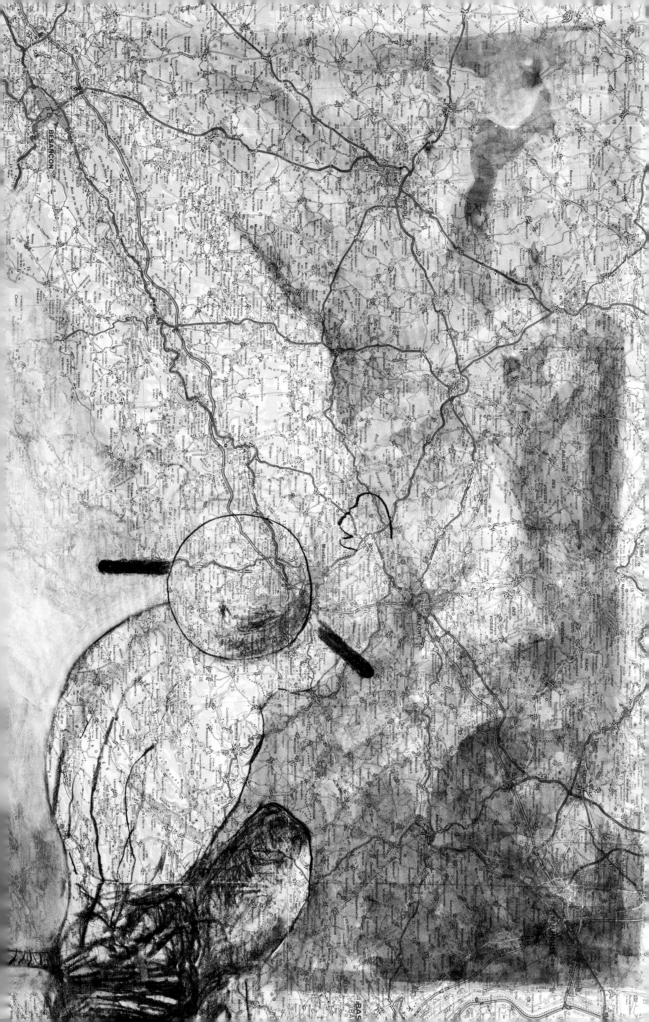

About the conversations

This series of letters began in January 2011 and continued until 2014, very much reflecting our work preoccupations and what was going on in our lives during that period. Although some sad personal events go unmentioned, it seems to me now that these letters became a way of addressing that other part of one's life that exists in parallel to the day-to-day; the life of the imagination and memory, of looking and making.

The layout presents the correspondence much as it was sent and received by the two of us and, I hope, conveys to the reader some of the pleasure and experience of opening those hand written letters from John in France and of making my side of the correspondence in the form of small books to send to him.
However frustrating the postal system can be, by turns annoyingly slow and, just occasionally, surprisingly fast, it still possesses a quality that email cannot have – the handling of the physical object.

With some small changes to accommodate copyright issues the layout remains faithful to the originals so that the reader will have the feeling of looking over our shoulders as each new letter presents itself.

Finally a quiet thought for three people to whom I would have liked to have shown the finished book:

Beverly Bancroft Berger 1942-2013
Dorothy Christie 1921-2015
Pep Subirós 1947-2016

Acknowledgements

There are a number of people I would like to thank who helped with advice, expertise and encouragement during the preparation of the book:

Martin Battye, Yves and Sandra Berger, Eulalia Bosch, Cathy Courtney, Gareth Evans, Joshua Gaskell, Amanda Geitner, Iona and David Heath, Eileen Hogan, Tom Overton, Rebecca Pickup, Anna Ridley, and Veronica Sekules.

Many thanks to the following who kindly gave permission to reproduce their own work or the work of others for inclusion in the book:

Gavin Bryars, Peter Foolen (Hans Waanders), Derrick and Sally Greaves (Prunella Clough), Markéta Luskačová, Maggi Hambling, Robert Macfarlane, Jean and Simone Mohr, Felicity Sparrow (Ian Breakwell) and Jill Turnbull (Gael Turnbull).

In addition to this book the *Lapwing and Fox* letters and related artworks also became the subject of an exhibition at the Sainsbury Centre for Visual Arts, Norwich (*Looking Beyond* 7th May-27th November 2016). The University of East Anglia postgraduate Museum Studies students curated the display under the guidance of their tutor Ed Krcma and I'd like to thank them all for their work putting this elegant exhibition together; Gabrielle Brasier, Sarah Coleman, Taryn Dennis, Rebecca Hirst, Rose Hughes, Gustav Imam, Hanna-Liis Kont, Ruth Law, Helen Martin, Imogen Phillips, Stephanie Santschi, Hollie Warman and Maria-Theresia Wehner, with special thanks going to Carolyn Addelman and Rebecca Hale who, in addition to their work in the curatorial team, helped me greatly with the copyright identification and administration for this book. They in turn were advised and guided in this task by Nell Croose-Myhill of SCVA who supported the project throughout.

I'd like to specially thank my wife Genevieve for her love and unfailing support, our daughter Alice who played her flute for the deer on that sunny Sunday in May 2012 and our son Theo who accompanied me on many of my walks on the footpaths around the wood. This book is for you.

It is also for Jonathan and Gemma and my grandchildren Kit and Coco, Rudi and Harvey, and for John's son Yves and grandchildren Mélina and Vincent.

Lastly, of course, my heartfelt thanks to John Berger himself for his friendship, encouragement and inspiration over the years since we first met in the early '80s, and for his readiness and enthusiasm to take an idea and steer it into a wider landscape.
John Christie June 2016

References, notes and bibliography

p.6 SURROUNDED BY FACES
At the book launch for *I Send You This Cadmium Red* in Barcelona in 2000 a member of the audience asked why grey was never chosen as one of the colours to write about and we explained that the correspondence hadn't started out with a set list and almost all the colours were there because they had presented themselves to us in one way or another, through books, quotations, exhibitions or everyday experiences – the colour grey had just never presented itself. The following morning we went, with our friend Eulalia Bosch, to an exhibition of Giacometti's work in La Pedrera, one of Gaudi's buildings on the Passeig de Gracia, and John spotted something. It was a quote from the artist answering the question as to why his later paintings seemed to avoid colour and tended towards grey? The essence of Giacometti's reply was that grey, in fact, contained all colours and for him 'signifies life itself''. JC

Hooper, S (1997). *Robert and Lisa Sainsbury Collection Vol 1-3.* Norwich: Yale University Press with University of East Anglia
Bonnefoy, Y (2000). *Giacometti.* Barcelona: Fundació Caixa Catalunya
Sylvester, D (1965). *Giacometti.* 2nd ed. London: Tate Gallery

p.32 ON HIS WAY SOMEWHERE ELSE
Hughes, R (1989). *Frank Auerbach.* London: Thames and Hudson
Lampert, C (1978). *Frank Auerbach.* London: Arts Council of Great Britain
Salvage of a Soho Photographer: The Life and Unsteady Times of John Deakin. dir: John Christie. Annalogue Productions for Channel Four Television (1991)

p.54 A SMALL GESTURE
Berger, J (1972). *G.* London: Weidenfeld and Nicolson
Berger, J (1994) *Pages of the Wound: Poems, Drawings, Photographs 1956-94* London: Circle Press
Hambling, M. Lambirth, A (2006) *Maggi Hambling The Works.* London: Unicorn Press
Hambling, M. (2001) *Father.* London: Morley Gallery
Danchev, A (2012). *George Braque: A Life.* New York: Arcade Publishing. p.259

p.76 A CIRCULAR WALK
The performance *Vanishing Points* with Anne Michaels at the German Gym, King's Cross was a part of the season *John Berger: Here Is Where We Meet* (11th April-18th May 2005) curated by Gareth Evans and presented at venues across London.

I showed my son Theo, who was nearly nine at the time, the postcard of Modigliani's *Anna Zborowski* (p.89) and asked him what he thought about it, what he could tell me about it, if anything. After considering the portrait he said he thought the shoulders were too different in height, that the hair looked a bit like a hat and her face and neck were too long. I was surprised he hadn't mentioned the eyes and asked him, had he any thoughts about the eyes?

He said, as if he hadn't mentioned it because it was too obvious, that she was probable blind, at least in one eye. JC

Bigsby, C (2001) *Writers in Conversation with Christopher Bigsby Vol.2* Norwich: Pen and Inc Press p.152
Michaels, A. Berger, J (2011). *Railtracks.* London: Go Together Press
Berger, J. Mohr, J (1982). *Another Way of Telling.* London: Writers & Readers
Another Way of Telling. (1988) dir: John Christie. Annalogue Productions for BBC Television
Spalding, F (2012). *Prunella Clough: Regions Unmapped.* London: Lund Humphries
Severini, G (1995). *The Life of a Painter.* New Jersey: Princeton University Press. p.48
Russoli, F (1959). *Modigliani.* London: Thames and Hudson
Russell, J (1963). *Modigliani.* London: The Arts Council

p.110 HIDING IN PLAIN VIEW
Berger, J (2011). *Bento's Sketchbook.* London: Verso
Williams, D (2001). *Naval Camouflage 1914-1945.* Rochester: Chatham Publishing
Blechman, H. Newman, A (2004). *DPM Disruptive Pattern Material.* London: DMP Ltd
Behrens, R (2002). *False Colors: Art, Design and Modern Camouflage.* Iowa: Bobolink Books
Forbes, P (2009). *Dazzled and Deceived.* London: Yale University Press
Lewison, J Ed. (1989). *A Genius of Industrial England, Edward Wadsworth.* Bradford: Arkwright Arts Trust
Glazebrook, M (1974). *Edward Wadsworth.* London: P & D Colnaghi
Morphet, R Ed. (1994). *R. B. Kitaj: A Retrospective.* London: Tate Gallery. p.216
Ríos, J (1994). *Kitaj: Pictures and Conversations.* London: Hamish Hamilton
Bown, S (2012). *The Last Viking: The Life of Roald Amundsen.* London: Aurum Press. p.319

p.146 LOOKING ON GLASS
Balcells, E, ed. Bosch, E (2012). *Años Luz (Light Years).* Madrid: Ministerio de Educación, Cultura y Deporte
Rowell, M (1979) *The Planar Dimension: Europe 1912-1932* University of Washington Press

p.172 AT A FRONTIER
Turnbull, G (2006) *There are words: Collected Poems.* Exeter: Sheersman Books
Turnbull, J & Whyte, H. (2012) *More Words: Gael Turnbull on Poets & Poetry.* Exeter: Sheersman Books
Heaney, S (1998). *Opened Ground.* London: Faber and Faber. p.169
Lingwood, J (1996). *Juan Muñoz.* Madrid: Museo Nacional Centro de Arte Reina Sofia
Severini, G (1995). *The Life of a Painter.* New Jersey: Princeton University Press. p.48
Macfarlane, R (2012). *The Old Ways.* London: Hamish Hamilton

p.206 NOT NATURE
Mandelstam, O, trans. McKane, R & E (2003). *The Moscow & Voronezh Notebooks*. Northumberland: Bloodaxe Books. p.125

p.234 REGARDING ANGELS
Rousseau, J-J tr. France, P (1974). *Reveries of the Solitary Walker*. London: Penguin
Sager, P (1994). *East Anglia: Essex, Suffolk & Norfolk*. London: Pallas Athene
Sebald, W. G (2002). *The Rings of Saturn*. London: Vintage,
Alsteens, S. Spira, S (2012). *Dürer and Beyond: Central European drawings, 1400-1700* New York: The Metropolitan Museum of Art
Serres, M (1993). *Angels: A Modern Myth*. Paris: Flammarion
Mercier, J, Lepage, C (2012). *Lalibela*. London: Peter Holberton Publishing
Ackroyd, P (1995). *Blake*. London: Sinclair-Stevenson. p360
Penrose, R (1958). *Picasso: His Life and Work*. London: Victor Gollancz. p.111

p.266 AN ATLAS FOR THE NEXT LIFE
At the beginning of our book *I Send You This Cadmium Red* there's a letter from John part of which says: 'I think that, in another life, I might be born in Barcelona, speaking Catalan. And you? Riga? Somewhere in the north of Canada? I don't know why I'm pushing you north, and I'm probably wrong. Where? Don't forget you'll need a basement for your presses. Let me know. Perhaps we could make a kind of atlas for the next life – with some fold-outs!' JC

Sebald, W.G (2011) *Austerlitz*. London: Penguin p.109
Daumier: Visions of Paris. London: Royal Academy of Arts (2013)
Waanders, H (2001). *Perches*. Eindhoven and Edinburgh: October/Morning Star
Waanders, H (2002). *Sealevel*. Eindhoven: October Foundation
Contributors: Finlay, A, Clark, T. A (2012). *Hans Waanders*. Small Publishers Fair London: Peter Foolen Editions
Bernstein, C (ed) (2006) *Louis Zukofsky Selected Poems*. New York: American Poets Project
Burton, R (2013) *A Strong Song Tows Us: The Life of Basil Bunting*. Oxford: Infinite Ideas Limited
Wings of Desire (Der Himmel über Berlin). dir: Wim Wenders (1987)

p.91. Amedeo Modigliani (1884-1920) *Portrait of a Woman (Anna Zborowska)* (detail)
France. *c.*1917. Pencil 47 × 30.2 cm.
Robert and Lisa Sainsbury Collection. UEA 15

p.93. Amedeo Modigliani (1884-1920) *Caryatid*
France. *c.*1913. Crayon and pencil 63.8 × 48.6 cm.
Robert and Lisa Sainsbury Collection. UEA 14

p.116. Prunella Clough (1919-1999) *Glove*
England. 1979. Glove on hessian and plaster.
Courtesy, Derrick and Sally Greaves
© Estate of Prunella Clough
All Rights Reserved, DACS 2016

p.129. Kitaj, Ronald Brooks (1932-2007): *Dismantling the Red Tent*, 1963-1964. Los Angeles (CA), Los Angeles County Museum of Art (LACMA). Oil and collage on canvas,122 × 122 cm. Michael & Dorothy Blankfort Bequest (AC1999.35.28) © 2016. Digital Image Museum Associates/LACMA/Art Resource NY/Scala, Florence

p.159. Jacob Epstein (1880-1959). *Head of an infant (Baby asleep)* England. c. 1902-04. Bronze, edition of 3 (?).
h. 10.4 × w. 13.8 × d. 11.5 cm.
Robert and Lisa Sainsbury Collection. UEA 75
© Tate, London

p.211. Juan Muñoz (1953-2001) *Many Times*,
Spain 1999 50 figures, polyester resin, fabric and pigment
Each figure approx.144 × 40 × 40 cm.
Courtesy of Juan Muñoz Estate and Marian Goodman Gallery.
© The Estate of Juan Muñoz. DACS 2016

p.215, 218. Ian Breakwell (1943-2005) *The Other Side*
England 2002 Video installation
Courtesy De La Warr Pavilion, Bexhill on Sea.
© The Estate of Ian Breakwell.
Courtesy Anthony Reynolds Gallery, London

p.222. John Christie (2012) *Overlappings 2 - Red/Yellow/Grey*
Pastel on paper 40 × 30cm

p.239. Hans Hoffmann (c.1530-1591/92) *A Hedgehog*
Germany before 1584. New York, Metropolitan Museum of Art. Watercolor and gouache on vellum. Sheet: 20.7 × 30.7 cm). Purchase, Annette de la Renta Gift, 2005 (2005.347). © 2016. Image copyright The Metropolitan Museum of Art/Art Resource/Scala, Florence

p.247. Markéta Luskačová, *Pilgrim*
Photograph. Courtesy of the artist

p.283. John Berger *Map trip*
Acrylic and graphite on printed road map 65 × 48cm

Photography credits

p.10, 11, 13, 18, 19, 23, 35, 37, 57, 81, 89, 91, 93 & 159.
Courtesy SCVA © James Austin
p.84(right) © Jean Mohr
p.115 © Cathy Courtney
p.129 © Photo SCALA, Florence
p.185 © Jill Turnbull
p.211 © Cathy Carver
p.212, 213 Courtesy Gavin Bryars
p.214 Courtesy De La Warr Pavilion
p.239 © Photo SCALA, Florence
p.249 © Markéta Luskačová
p.275, 276 (bottom) © Hans Waanders
p.276 (top) © Peter Foolen
p.9, 10 (bottom left), 11(right), 15, 17, 20-22, 41-44, 90, 94, 116, 123-5, 127,131, 133, 150, 156-8, 175, 177, 179, 187, 197, 214, 217, 218-9, 241, 243, 245, 248, 271, 274, 279. © JC

Every effort has been made to trace copyright holders. In the case of an error or omission, the publisher is happy to correct any details in subsequent editions.

John Berger is a novelist, essayist, art critic, poet and artist. His many novels include the Booker Prize-winner *G* (1972), his critically acclaimed trilogy *Into Their Labour* (1991) and *From A to X* (2008). His books on art and photography include *Ways of Seeing* (1972) an influential text and series of films for BBC TV, *The Success and Failure of Picasso* (1965), *The Shape of a Pocket* (2001) and *Bento's Sketchbook* (2011). John Berger lives and works in Paris.

John Christie is an artist, film-maker and publisher with artwork in public and private collections worldwide. He has collaborated with John Berger on a number of projects including *Another Way of Telling*, a series of four films he directed and photographed for BBC TV (1988). He designed and published *Pages of the Wound* (1994), John Berger's book of poems, drawings and photographs and co-wrote *I Send You This Cadmium Red* (2000) their book of correspondence on the subject of colour.
John Christie lives and works in Suffolk, East Anglia.

First published in 2016 by OBJECTIF

Text copyright © John Berger and John Christie 2016
The moral right of the authors has been asserted.
Copyright of quotations used within the text remain with the original author

Design and layout copyright © OBJECTIF 2016
Parham House Barn, Brick Lane, Framlingham, Suffolk IP13 9LQ
www.objectifpress.co.uk
john@objectifpress.co.uk

A CIP record for this book is available from the British Library.

Set in Gill Sans and Courier New
Printed on 115gsm G Print SRA2

Book design: John Christie
Thanks to Dean Hearn at Healeys for his careful work on the picture scans
Printed and bound in Suffolk by Healeys Print Group, Ipswich

ISBN 978-1-5262-0473-8

LOTTERY FUNDED   Supported using public funding by
ARTS COUNCIL ENGLAND